Paving With Pervious Concrete

George Garber

Schiffer Publishing Ltd ®

4880 Lower Valley Road Atglen, Pennsylvania 19310

Schiffer Books are available at special discounts for bulk
purchases for sales promotions or premiums. Special editions,
including personalized covers, corporate imprints, and
excerpts can be created in large quantities for special needs.
For more information contact the publisher:

Published by Schiffer Publishing Ltd.
4880 Lower Valley Road
Atglen, PA 19310
Phone: (610) 593-1777; Fax: (610) 593-2002
E-mail: Info@schifferbooks.com

For the largest selection of fine reference books on this and
related subjects, please visit our web site at:
www.schifferbooks.com
We are always looking for people to write books on new and
related subjects. If you have an idea for a book please contact
us at the above address.

This book may be purchased from the publisher.
Include $5.00 for shipping.
Please try your bookstore first.
You may write for a free catalog.

In Europe, Schiffer books are distributed by
Bushwood Books
6 Marksbury Ave.
Kew Gardens
Surrey TW9 4JF England
Phone: 44 (0) 20 8392 8585; Fax: 44 (0) 20 8392 9876
E-mail: info@bushwoodbooks.co.uk
Website: www.bushwoodbooks.co.uk

Contents

Acknowledgments

Like almost everyone else in the field, I didn't learn about pervious concrete in school. My teachers were other writers and concrete workers. Most of the writers are named here under References. I won't name the workers — in many cases I never learned their names — but they were no less important.

Among the dozens who helped me, four deserve special mention.

Bruce Ferguson wrote the defining book on pervious pavements (not just those made of concrete). His *Porous Pavements* is a gold mine of information.

Alan Sparkman at the Tennessee Concrete Association provided technical information and a long list of pervious pavements for me to visit. He is a highly persuasive salesperson for pervious concrete, but at the same time he keeps an open mind about its limitations and the variety of ways to make and use it. That's a rare and refreshing combination.

Tina Skinner at Schiffer Publishing planted the seed for this book. Though I had first encountered pervious concrete more than two decades before I met her, she was the one who opened my eyes to the growing interest in it and persuaded me the subject justified a new book.

Above all I thank Carol — my wife, chief editor, and traveling companion. She has seen almost as many pervious-concrete pavements as I have, and I know she looks forward to the day when we can take a car trip without my saying, "Uh, there's this pervious job I'd like to check out."

Chapter 1
The Concrete with Holes

Rain. It brings life, and it brings death and destruction. On the one hand it waters forests, farms, and lawns. It turns the prairie green and makes the desert bloom. On the other hand it causes rivers to rise out of their banks, flooding houses and sweeping people to their deaths. It washes pollutants into waterways. It ponds on roads and paths, making travel more dangerous.

Whether rain does good or harm depends, to a large extent, on the sort of terrain it falls on. Where the ground is impervious, water either ponds on top or, more often, runs off quickly into streams and rivers where it contributes to flooding and pollution. But where the ground is pervious, rainwater soaks in. It is then available to support plant growth and to recharge underground aquifers. Much of the water eventually enters the surface drainage system, but it does so slowly and gently, avoiding the extremes of high and low flow that occur in areas of impervious ground.

This healthy stream flows through an area of pervious surfaces, including a path made of pervious concrete.

Modern highways cover huge swathes of countryside with impervious concrete and asphalt.

The natural world contains both pervious and impervious surfaces, but the pervious ones dominate the scene. Forests, meadows, and prairies all absorb most of the rain that falls on them. Bare rock and solid ice are impervious, but they aren't common in the regions where most people live. Nature often covers even relatively impervious soils, such as clays, with a humus-rich topsoil layer that absorbs water.

In contrast, the manmade world is loaded with impervious surfaces, and their extent grows daily. Almost every building has an impervious roof. Roads, parking lots, and footpaths are paved with impervious concrete and asphalt.

Modern industrial societies cover prodigious amounts of their territory with impervious materials. In the United States, each mile of four-lane, interstate highway puts dense concrete or asphalt on top of 9.2 acres (2.3 hectares per kilometer) of landscape, most of which used to be pervious. If the highway is six lanes wide, as many now are, the paved area goes up to 12.1 acres per mile (3.0 hectares per kilometer). Shopping malls are surrounded by thousands of parking spaces, almost all paved in asphalt. Houses not only have impervious roofs, but also include paved driveways, patios, and footpaths. The area of outdoor paving often exceeds the house's actual footprint. City parks offer some respite from all that pavement, but even they contain roads, parking lots, and paved areas for sports like basketball and tennis.

This degraded urban stream takes in polluted runoff from impervious streets, sidewalks, and driveways. A natural, year-round waterway once flowed here.

There is another way, however. Pavements need not be impervious. We can make many of them pervious instead, using materials that do not block water. When rain falls on pervious pavement it goes right through and enters the ground. Nature then takes care of the water much as it did before the area was paved.

The list of pervious paving materials includes porous asphalt, certain block pavers, grass grids, unbound aggregate, and mulch. All have their uses, and we will look at them in chapter 3. But of all the possible materials, the most promising and most versatile is this book's subject: pervious concrete.

What is it?

Everyday concrete — called dense concrete when we need to distinguish it from the pervious kind — contains four key ingredients: stone, sand, cement, and water. Stone, also called coarse aggregate, consists of rock particles at least 3/16 inch (5 mm) across. Sand, also called fine aggregate, consists of rock particles cement less than 3/16 inch (5 mm) across. Cement is Portland cement, a powder that hardens into a rocklike mass when mixed with water. It is made from limestone and clay that are heated almost to the melting point, then cooled and ground into dust. Water is just water.

Dense concrete contains a wide range of particle sizes. The smaller particles fill the gaps between the bigger ones. Cement paste fills the gaps between the smaller particles, creating a dense, impervious mass.

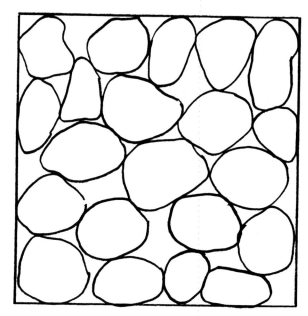

Pervious concrete contains big particles and cement paste. The connected gaps between the big particles make the material pervious. Cement paste coats the particles but does not fill the gaps.

Ordinary dense concrete is highly impervious to water.

When we mix stone, sand, cement, and water in the right proportions, we end up with concrete, an amazingly useful material. Ordinary concrete is strong, hard, durable, cheap, and capable of being formed into many shapes — all desirable properties. But it has one other property we don't always want. It is relatively impervious to liquids.

I say "relatively" because concrete isn't really waterproof, as many an owner of a damp basement can attest. Water can enter through cracks and through the microscopic pores that are always present. Still, concrete resists water well enough that we use it for dams and canal locks.

But we can change that by taking out one of concrete's basic ingredients — the sand. The result, called no-fines concrete, pervious concrete, or porous concrete, is full of interconnected voids. The voids make up from 15 to 40% of the concrete's total volume. Water flows freely through those voids, even where the void percentage is near the low end of the range.

Pervious concrete consists of coarse aggregate, cement, and water. It often contains other things as well: chemical admixtures, pozzolans, or fibers. Nowadays many pervious-concrete mixes include a little sand, and for that reason the old name, no-fines concrete, isn't as accurate as it used to be. But those extra ingredients don't change the basic structure: pebbles glued to one another with cement, with lots of holes.

How pervious is it?

If not sealed or clogged, pervious concrete has an infiltration rate of 670 to 900 in./hr (17,000 to 22,900 mm/hr) (Ferguson 2005, 124). To put that another way, a square foot of good pervious concrete can take in at least 418 gallons of water an hour, or 7 gallons a minute.

That's pervious indeed. Rainfall rates don't reach those numbers anywhere on the planet. Even a blinding rain, such as a hurricane might produce, rarely exceeds 3 in./hr (75 mm/hr).

Pervious concrete infiltrates water faster than any natural soil, and beats all other construction materials except unbound aggregate, which goes up to about 50,000 in./hr (1270 mm/hr) per hour for 1-in. (25-mm) material. The following table shows infiltration rates for some common surfaces:

This pervious-concrete mix contains nothing but coarse aggregate, cement, and water.

Dense concrete on the left, pervious on the right.

Infiltration rates (Ferguson 2005, 124 and 144)

Surface	in./hr	mm/hr
Dense concrete	<0.00002	<0.005
Dense asphalt	0.00006-6	0.002-150
Clay soil	0.02	0.5
Clay loam soil	0.09	2.3
Turf	0.2-3.9	5-99
Loam soil	0.52	13
Sandy loam soil	1.02	25.9
Loamy sand soil	2.41	61.2
Sandy soil	8.27	210
Forest soil	8-60	200-1500
Pervious asphalt	170-500	4,300-12,700
Pervious concrete	670-900	17,000-22,860
1/4-in. (6-mm) unbound aggregate	1,500	38,100
1/2-in. (13-mm) unbound aggregate	2,500	63,500
1-in, (25-mm) unbound aggregate	50,000	1,270,000

If pervious concrete is sealed by overcompaction or troweling during construction, its infiltration rate drops sharply — down to as little as 1.25 in./hr (32 mm/hr). But that's still higher than most other materials.

Infiltration rates don't tell the whole story, however. Some water can run off even where the measured infiltration rate exceeds the rainfall rate. That's because the tests for infiltration do not exactly duplicate what happens in a real rainstorm (Ferguson 2005, 126). Another property, called the runoff coefficient, more accurately predicts how much rain will run off.

The runoff coefficient is the measured surface runoff divided by the rainfall, and it ranges from 0 (nothing running off) to 1 (everything running off). According to Ferguson, no standard value has yet been determined for pervious concrete's runoff coefficient, but it "would presumably be comparable to that of porous asphalt" (Ferguson 2005, 126). Porous asphalt's runoff coefficient ranges from 0.12 to 0.40. In contrast, dense concrete's runoff coefficient ranges from 0.75 to 0.97, and that for turf ranges from 0.05 to 0.53.

Engineering properties

Despite its porosity, pervious concrete is still concrete. It should come as no surprise that it has engineering properties similar to those of dense concrete. Differences exist, however, and they can be substantial. Some of the differences favor dense concrete, while some go the other way.

Strength

Concrete is often identified by its compressive strength. This is its resistance to crushing, measured by squeezing a cylinder of the material till it breaks. Some countries test cubes instead of cylinders. Pervious concrete has less compressive strength than dense concrete made with a similar amount of cement. However, quite a range is possible, and the strength ranges for dense and pervious concretes overlap. Compressive strengths for dense concrete, at least for the mixes used in paving, range from 2500 to 6000 psi (17 to 40 MPa). For pervious concrete the range runs from 400 to 4000 psi (3 to 28 MPa).

Though compressive strength is what everybody looks at (because it's easy to measure), flexural strength is what really matters in pavement design. Flexural strength is resistance to bending, measured by applying bending force to a test beam 6 x 6 x 24 in. (150 x 150 x 600 mm). Pervious concrete's flexural strength ranges from 150 to 600 psi (1 to 4 MPa).

Dense concrete's strength depends on its mix design — mainly its cement content and water-cement ratio. Pervious concrete's strength depends largely on how well it's compacted. Mix design matters, but mainly because of its effect on compaction. Adding cement to pervious concrete will not always make it stronger.

Because strength depends so much on compaction, it may not be uniform through the full depth of the slab. Compaction is generally better at the top (Delatte 2007, 69). Presumably strength is, too.

Drying shrinkage

All concrete shrinks as it dries, and that shrinkage can cause cracks. Pervious concrete reportedly shrinks only about half as much as dense concrete (Tennis, 6). This difference results in fewer drying-shrinkage cracks, reduced crack width, and reduced need for crack-control joints. Many pervious-concrete pavements are built with no crack-control joints and are just allowed to crack.

In the absence of test data, it's reasonable to assume a drying-shrinkage rate of 0.02 to 0.03% (Murdock 1991, 384).

Density (unit weight)

Pervious concrete always weighs less than dense concrete made with the same coarse aggregate, because so much of it consists of air. The reduction in density closely matches the void content.

Dense concrete without entrained air and with normal-weight aggregates weighs about 145 lb/cu ft (2300 kg/cu m). A comparable pervious concrete with 20% voids weighs about 116 lb/cu ft (1,840 kg/cu m). The density itself rarely matters, but it's often measured as a proxy for void content, which does matter.

Pervious concrete's unit weight puts it in the category of lightweight concrete. The more usual way to make lightweight concrete is to use lightweight aggregates, but the voids in pervious concrete have a similar effect. Though unimportant in pavement design, the lighter weight might offer advantages in other fields.

Void content

This is a key property of pervious concrete, and also applies to aggregates used in sub-bases. It's the volume of voids (spaces available to be filled with air or water) divided by the total volume of concrete, expressed as a percentage. Void contents range from 15 to 40%. Concrete with less than 15% voids is possible, but it may not have enough permeability to qualify as pervious. Void contents much above 40% are impossible with normally-shaped aggregates.

Void content is pervious concrete's essential property, but you can have too much of a good thing. Higher void content means greater permeability and more reservoir capacity — both desirable. But it also means lower strength and more raveling, which are not what you want.

Void contents have trended lower over the years. A roadway described in 1970 reportedly had 40% voids (Maynard 1970). You can't get much higher than that. Percentages in the mid-twenties have been common in recent years. But some people are pushing for lower void contents, sometimes as low as 16%.

Void content depends on the aggregate gradation and shape, and on the degree of compaction. The highest void contents are achieved with single-size, angular aggregates and minimal compaction.

There is no practical way to measure the void content of fresh concrete. Density is normally measured instead, since it is closely tied to void content and is easy to measure. Once the concrete has hardened, you can confirm void content directly.

A sample of known volume is weighed to determine the concrete's density.

History

Pervious concrete is older than many people realize. That's something to keep in mind when skeptics say it's too new for us to have confidence in its properties.

I've heard, but cannot verify, that concrete was made without sand in the nineteenth century. Regardless of that claim, the material's record definitely goes back at least to 1953, when the American Concrete Institute published an article about what it called "no-fines concrete," including details on strength and density (Valore 1951).

In the 1970s, if not earlier, Europeans built walls of no-fines concrete for houses and apartment buildings. The builders weren't interested in the material's pervious nature, however. On the contrary, they waterproofed the walls on the outside, and plastered them on the inside. No-fines concrete was used in walls for its lighter weight and better insulating value, compared to dense concrete.

The Europeans did not fail to notice, however, that no-fines concrete let water pass through, and that such a property could be useful in pavements. An especially interesting experiment took place in 1970 or slightly earlier, when a public road in Nottinghamshire, England, was paved with a pervious-concrete topping (Maynard 1970). In 1976 and 1980 the UK's Cement and Concrete Association (C&CA) published guides to the construction of sports facilities, with detailed recommendations for pavements made of pervious concrete (Enoch 1976 and 1980). During the 1970s and 1980s the C&CA vigorously promoted pervious concrete for sports surfaces because water did not pond on it. In 1984 I saw a pervious tennis court at the C&CA's old headquarters (since sold off) in Wexham Springs. It was then several years old and partly clogged with leaf litter, but it still drained well and looked good.

The builders of those early British pavements liked pervious concrete mainly for its ability to prevent ponding. They weren't focusing on its hydrologic benefits.

In contrast, the rise of pervious concrete in Florida a few years later resulted directly from that state's problems with stormwater. Florida gets a lot of rain, much of it in heavy, intense storms. The natural landscape has considerable ability to handle that rain, since the state has highly pervious, sandy soils. But that ability vanishes when you cover the ground with impervious pavement. And covering sand with pavement was exactly what Floridians were doing, faster than almost anyone else in America.

Jack Paine may have been the first to recognize that Florida in the 1970s made a near-perfect candidate for pervious concrete paving (Ferguson 2005, 419). The population was growing fast. Stormwater problems were getting worse. Underground aquifers essential for drinking water and irrigation were shrinking. The mild climate eliminated the risk of frost damage (more on that later). And the ground's natural porosity made hydrologic design simple, with little need for sub-bases and drains.

By the turn of the twenty-first century Florida led the United States, and probably the world, in both the amount of pervious concrete on the ground and the understanding of how to place it. But interest was already moving north, first to Georgia, then to the mid-South, and eventually to states and provinces across North America.

This geographic spread did not occur without opposition. Many people feared that a technology developed in Florida's warm climate and suited for Florida's free-draining sands wouldn't fare well in the harsher environment of the Northeast and Midwest, to say nothing of Canada. The opposition has faded as pervious concrete pavements proved durable, at least for several years, in places such as northern Illinois, central Pennsylvania, and the high desert of New Mexico.

As I write this in 2009, pervious concrete pavements are working well in dozens of US states and several Canadian provinces. Several organizations are teaching contractors how to place pervious concrete, while the Portland Cement Association and the National Ready Mix Concrete Association promote its use.

That all sounds impressive. And yet it must be said that pervious concrete remains a niche product, making up only a minuscule fraction of the total paved area. Most pervious projects have been, to some extent, experiments or showpieces. Almost all were built for public institutions or non-profit corporations, and not for businesses or individuals spending their own money. You might run into pervious concrete at a library or city park. You almost certainly won't see it in front of a strip mall out on the bypass. For several years advocates have claimed that wide adoption of pervious concrete lay right around the corner, but that corner never seemed to get any closer.

But we may finally have reached that corner. Pervious concrete usage is undeniably rising, and I believe it is close to a tipping point, beyond which it will become much more popular, more widely accepted, and cheaper.

Whether I am right or wrong about the tipping point, the concrete with holes in it has a role — indeed several roles — to play. We'll look at them in the next chapter.

Chapter 2
Why and Where to Use
Pervious Concrete

"When it rains, it drains." That's more than a cute slogan used by promoters. It explains, in five words, pervious concrete's main reason for existence.

Water ponds on dense concrete.

When rain falls on impervious surfaces such as dense concrete or ordinary asphalt, it either ponds on top or runs off. Both outcomes cause problems. Ponding is a nuisance, and becomes a hazard if the water freezes or if fast motor traffic crosses it. Runoff increases flooding and water pollution, and its control requires costly measures such as storm sewers and detention ponds.

But when rain falls on pervious concrete, it sinks in. Ponding is just about eliminated. Runoff is greatly reduced and more easily controlled.

On the face of it, then, pervious concrete seems to be a good choice for any pavement that gets rained on. But of course it is not that simple, or else we would see it on every street. Pervious concrete works superbly in some situations. In other cases it is a reasonable option but needs to be weighed against the alternatives — and there are always alternatives. And in some places it should not be used at all.

In this chapter we will examine the reasons people use pervious concrete, and consider the sorts of jobs it is suited for. In Chapter 3 we will look at the arguments against it, and at some of the alternatives to it.

Benefits

Pervious concrete's big benefits center on how it handles water. Other benefits are marginal, at least in pavements. The water-related benefits include stormwater control, filtration, and the elimination of ponding. The other, lesser benefits include its light color, light weight, and thermal insulating properties.

Stormwater control

The current interest in pervious concrete focuses on stormwater control. Stormwater in this context includes all the liquid water that gets dumped on the ground; it is not limited to the sort of storm that sinks ships and topples trees. In some climates the greatest stormwater flows come not from rain, but from the spring snowmelt.

Stormwater problems grow as impervious surfaces cover more and more of our landscape. Water runs off instead of soaking into the ground. Creeks and rivers flood more often and rise higher. Storm sewers — and sometimes sanitary sewers, too — are overloaded.

And it's not just that the problems are getting worse. Standards are getting stricter. Governments forbid construction practices that were normal a generation ago. Regulations differ from place to place, but the intent — if not always the result — is to ensure that construction does not create or worsen stormwater problems downstream.

On almost any project, replacing impervious pavement with pervious concrete will reduce runoff and lower the peak stormwater flow from the site. With the right hydrologic design, a pervious pavement can even absorb runoff from nearby impervious pavements and roofs, neutralizing their ill effect.

Pervious concrete is not the only solution to stormwater problems, of course. It's not even the most popular solution. That would be to stick with impervious paving materials while directing runoff to a soakaway, detention pond, or retention pond, where it can soak into the ground or discharge slowly into the surface drainage system. A soakaway is a covered hole, usually filled with loose aggregate. Detention and retention ponds are depressions in the ground that fill with stormwater. A detention pond normally stays dry and contains water only briefly. In contrast, a retention pond is designed to hold some water even during dry spells. (People confuse the two, as did I till I remembered that dry and detention both start with the letter d.)

The popular solution is far from perfect, however. Soakaway are largely limited to small sites. Detention ponds and retention ponds can be designed to handle runoff from the biggest sites, but they take a lot of room. Some North American cities have hundreds of detention ponds (retention ponds are scarcer) taking up many acres of land. The best of them support some vegetation and a little recreational use. The worst are eyesores — trash pits in dry weather, mud holes in wet, ringed by chain link fencing and "keep out" signs.

Pervious paving, with good hydrologic design, eliminates the need for most soakaways and ponds. Even if they are still needed, as is sometimes the case where the ground under the pavement has a low infiltration rate, they can be made smaller and cheaper. The money saved by eliminating costly drainage features often exceeds the extra cost of the pervious concrete itself.

Ponding

Rainwater and snowmelt often pond on top of dense concrete and asphalt pavements. Ponding is both dangerous and annoying.

The dangers include:

- hydroplaning, which can cause fast motor vehicles to skid and crash;
- blinding spray thrown up by motor vehicles, especially big trucks;
- worse night-time visibility;
- hiding of potholes;
- ice.

Except for ice, which endangers every user, the risks of ponding occur mainly on roads that get fast motor traffic.

Not every detention pond is as ugly as this one, next to a busy street in Lexington, Kentucky. Then again, some look even worse. Pervious concrete eliminates the need for detention ponds on many sites.

Up to now few such roads have been made of pervious concrete, but that could change.

The nuisance factor applies to all kinds of traffic. Nobody, except school kids on their bikes, enjoys traveling through a puddle.

You can slope an impervious surface to prevent ponding, but that complicates construction and isn't always effective. Specifications and codes often call for a 2% slope to prevent ponding, but you really need 3% or more to be reasonably sure of success. Sports surfaces pose a special problem in this regard, because some games require a pavement that is close to level. I hear that some tennis-court owners keep squeegees on hand to push the water off after a rain.

Pervious concrete almost wholly eliminates ponding, and you need not slope it. Even a thin topping of pervious concrete, which wouldn't do much for stormwater control, drains fast after the heaviest rains.

Filtration

Besides regulating water's flow, pervious concrete can improve its quality.

Water falls from the sky clean enough to drink but it doesn't stay that way. Once it reaches the ground it picks up a variety of pollutants, including animal waste, plant debris, and motor oil. When the water runs off an impervious surface, all those pollutants go with it into rivers and lakes.

In contrast, pervious concrete removes and processes some of those pollutants. Solids tend to stay on top of the pavement, where they can be cleaned up later or will decompose as they are exposed to sunshine and

Water has ponded on the asphalt, but not on the pervious concrete. This is a parking lot at Middle Tennessee State University in Murfreesboro.

From left to right: dense asphalt, dense concrete, and pervious concrete. Note that the pervious concrete is darker than the dense concrete, but lighter than the asphalt. This is a parking lot at Milton Middle School in Milton, West Virginia.

air. (However, some solids stick in the concrete's pores, causing clogs, and that's not so good.) Liquid pollutants and fine suspended particles can pass through the pavement, of course, but some of them are digested by the bacteria that take up residence there. At least one company even sells bacteria to get the process started.

The use of pervious concrete in livestock facilities relies heavily on its filtration abilities.

Bear in mind, though, that filtration through pervious concrete is not a cure-all for water pollution problems. It will not replace septic fields and sewage treatment plants. Still, when it comes to controlling water pollution, every little bit helps, and pervious concrete helps a little bit.

Mitigation of heat islands

A heat island is an artificially warm area, normally associated with a big city. It arises because buildings and pavements heat up on sunny days, absorbing more solar radiation than do the surrounding natural surfaces. Heat produced directly by human activity, called anthropogenic heat, also plays a role in the formation of heat islands, though it's much smaller. Global warming is not an issue here; heat islands are local, not global.

Some people claim that pervious concrete can reduce the absorption that creates heat islands. To judge that claim we have to ask: compared to what?

These trees are thriving amid pervious concrete in Williamsburg, Virginia.

Materials vary greatly in the amount of heat they absorb from the sun. Lighter-colored materials tend to absorb less, though that's an imperfect guide since much of the sun's radiation is invisible. The standard measure is the solar reflectance index, or SRI (ASTM E 1980). This takes into account both reflectance (the material's ability to reflect solar radiation) and emittance (the material's ability to get rid of heat once it has been absorbed). The SRI scale runs from 0 to 1, where 0 represents the value for a standard black surface, and 1 represents a standard white. New asphalt pavements have SRI readings near zero. Dense-concrete pavements are brighter, with readings from 35 to 55 when new. Readings above 80 are possible with white Portland cement or white paint. The gap between asphalt and concrete narrows over time, with asphalt growing lighter and concrete darker. But even in old pavements concrete is brighter.

When you are trying to reduce heat islands, higher SRI readings are better. A key number is 0.29, because that's the point at which a pavement qualifies for LEED credit. Dense concrete reliably comes in above 0.29, at least when new. Asphalt never does, unless you add reflective material to it. Pervious concrete falls in the middle. It often measures above 0.29, but you can't count on that.

You can raise pervious concrete's SRI by using slag — ground granulated blast furnace slag — to replace some of the Portland cement. A typical slag mix will have a cementitious component that is 30% slag, 70% Portland. Using white Portland cement instead of the usual grey will lighten the finished product even more, but that stuff costs a fortune.

If we look only at SRI, then, pervious concrete seems to offer only modest help in the fight against heat islands. It beats asphalt but comes in behind dense concrete. There is one more piece to the puzzle, however. Trees mitigate the heat-island effect. And pervious pavements are more compatible with tree growth.

Benefits outside the paving field

Pervious concrete has a few properties that don't matter in pavements, but can be beneficial when the material is used for other purposes. Compared to dense concrete, pervious weighs less, insulates better, and transmits less moisture through capillary action.

Pervious concrete is a form of lightweight concrete, though we don't usually describe it in those terms. The reduction in weight is almost exactly equal to the void content. If concrete has 20% voids, it is going to weigh about 20% less. Some of the early research into no-fines concrete focused more on its light weight than on its pervious qualities (Valore, 1951).

Materials full of air voids tend to be good at thermal insulation, and pervious concrete is no exception. Its thermal conductivity is about half that of dense concrete (Murdock, 1991, 384).

My comment that pervious concrete transmits less moisture through capillary action may seem pointless, if not ludicrous. After all, easy transmission of water is exactly what pervious concrete is famous for — in pavements. But if you are building a wall, the outside will be covered to keep rain out, and then the lack of capillary action will stop moisture from being drawn in (Murdock, 1991, 388).

How green is my concrete?

Pervious concrete's current appeal owes a lot — almost everything, in fact — to its status as a green building material. People like it because they think it is easy on the environment. Stormwater control, water filtration, and heat islands are all environmental issues, and are all areas where pervious concrete offers benefits.

LEED certification

In the United States, a construction material's environmental reputation is closely tied to LEED certification. LEED stands for Leadership in Energy and Environmental Design. Run by the United States Green Building Council, the LEED certification program assigns points for construction practices and materials that reduce harm to the environment. The current system, subject to change, allows a maximum of 110 points. LEED basic certification requires at least 40 points. Higher certifications are possible: silver for 50 to 59 points, gold for 60 to 79, and platinum for 80 and above. Certification applies not to individual materials but to the whole project, which typically consists of a building and the site on which it stands. Some owners demand LEED certification (usually at the basic level) for their projects.

Pervious concrete offers several opportunities for earning LEED credit (Ashley, 82-84), though rarely would all be available on a single job. The opportunities include:

- stormwater management;
- reduction of heat-island effect by using materials with SRI (surface reflectance index) of 29 or higher;
- use of recycled materials;
- use of local materials;
- harvesting of stormwater for landscape irrigation.

As useful as the certification program can be, we should remember that LEED and green are not synonyms. You can build in an environmentally responsible way without participating in LEED certification.

Avoiding the hype

If you believed the claims made by its more extreme promoters, you'd think pervious concrete was the greenest building material around. Apparently we need only bulldoze what's left of the rain forest, pave it all with pervious concrete, and our problems will be solved.

But of course it's not that simple. It's not simple at all, if you seriously want to minimize harm to the environment.

People considering pervious concrete for its green benefits tend to fall into two groups. The first group, to which nobody admits belonging, doesn't really care about the environment but wants to be seen as caring, if that's what the game calls for. Members of this group don't agonize over whether to use pervious concrete. If it meets the code or provides the LEED credit they seek, that's good enough.

The other group truly wants what is best for the environment. Members of this group have their work cut out for them, because no building material or method is wholly green. Some are greener than others, but it can be hard to tell.

Suppose you've narrowed the candidates down to dense versus pervious concrete. Pervious is the obvious choice there, right?

Well, maybe not. What if you're building a heavily used road, where pervious concrete would fail in a few years but dense concrete would last decades? What if you're renovating an old factory site where the ground could be contaminated? In both situations you could make a good case for dense concrete as the greener choice.

In the end there is no substitute for careful analysis and some hard thinking. Sometimes pervious concrete will be the right choice. Sometimes it won't be. While I can't do that analysis and thinking for you, I can offer a few suggestions:

> The greenest pavement is usually the smallest. Almost anything you can do to reduce the pavement's area, or the volume of material in it, will lessen the effect on the environment.

> Among the pervious materials, turf, unbound aggregate, and mulch tend to be greener than pervious concrete, pervious asphalt, or pervious pavers. But don't forget the next point.

> Consider life-cycle costs. No pavement lasts forever. At some point it will need to be replaced, or renovated, or removed and disposed of. All those options involve environmental costs. Life-cycle accounting allows for the costs of making, using, maintaining, and eventually disposing of the pavement.

> Cheaper frequently means greener. The choice that costs less tends to be easier on the environment. This is not an infallible rule, especially where novel materials and methods are involved, but it's usually true. The forester and naturalist Mollie Beattie said: "If it's un-environmental it is uneconomical. That is the rule of nature." However, she wasn't talking just about the dollar amount on the contractor's check. For a complete economic comparison, we have to consider life-cycle costs and add in externalities such as pollution caused by manufacture of building materials.

Typical uses

Pervious concrete has been used, and is worth considering, for all these uses:

- sidewalks and footpaths;
- shared-use paths;
- driveways;
- parking lots;
- patios and plazas;
- sports surfaces;
- streets and roads;
- livestock facilities;
- non-pavement applications.

Sidewalks and footpaths

These are meant for foot traffic only. They don't support motor vehicles, except where they cross driveways. While they may see the occasional bicycle, that's not their purpose and they need not be designed for bikes.

The sidewalk is a special kind of footpath. Located in the public right of way, it is subject to laws and customs that don't apply to other footpaths. Most cities and towns regulate their sidewalks, laying down rules for location, width, thickness, gradient, and composition. It's the rules on composition that are most likely to give you grief, because few were written with pervious concrete in mind. In recent years some communities have specifically endorsed, or at least allowed, pervious concrete in their sidewalk regulations. Their numbers will grow. Meanwhile, don't give up if your town's officials aren't among the enlightened ones. You stand a good chance of getting a variance if you explain the merits of pervious concrete. You could show them this book, for a start.

Are sidewalks and footpaths a good fit for pervious concrete? Generally they are, with one caveat we'll get to later. It's easy to make them out of pervious concrete, even with hand tools. And light-duty paths get around some of the doubts people have as to pervious concrete's ability to handle heavy loads and abrasive traffic.

Pervious concrete makes a good surface for walking, though wearers of high-heel shoes might prefer something smoother. Some people say it feels softer underfoot than dense concrete. It isn't really softer, of course, but it may feel softer because of the way the pebbly surface interacts with soft soles.

The caveat I mentioned? Sidewalks and footpaths are generally too small to take full advantage of pervious concrete's benefits. Truth be told, narrow paths are not huge contributors to runoff and pollution. If the only pavements on earth were footpaths, no one would need pervious concrete.

Shared-use paths

Also known as multi-use paths, these support a traffic mix that includes walkers, runners, wheelchair users, and bicyclists. It's the addition of cyclists that make multi-use paths different from footpaths. Though public motor vehicles are banned, many shared-use paths see occasional motor traffic by emergency workers and maintenance crews.

Shared-use paths look like footpaths. But mainly because of their bicycle traffic, they are designed more like roads. You have to consider lane widths, sight distances, the radius of curves, and whether to bank the curves. For help with all that, consult AASHTO's Guide for the Development of Bicycle Facilities (AASHTO, 1999).

Pervious concrete works well for many shared-use paths, but not all.

Paths used for horseback riding are not, as a rule, good candidates for pervious concrete. Equestrians prefer unpaved surfaces and aren't comfortable sharing the road with cyclists — who generally prefer pavement. Paths meant for riding — bridle paths — are better left unpaved. Reserve pervious concrete for the paths that see more bikes than horses.

A sidewalk in Knoxville, Tennessee

Not all cyclists like pervious concrete paths, however. The pebbly texture can irritate cyclists who ride racing-style machines with narrow, high-pressure tires. In practice this issue turns out to matter less than you might suspect, because the people who ride those bikes are not the main users of shared-use paths. They tend to stick to roads where they can ride fast without interference from slow cyclists and pedestrians.

Roller skaters also find pervious concrete too rough. Whether you consider this a drawback or an advantage depends on how you feel about skaters on shared-use paths. Some managers are happy to discourage them.

Because shared-use paths are typically just wide enough to support a car or pickup truck, they run the risk of damage when emergency or maintenance crews (or trespassers) drive on them. The motor vehicle's tires run close to the slab's edges, where it is least able to support them without breaking. Proposed solutions to this problem include widening the pavement to 10 ft (3.0 m) and stabilizing the shoulders (AASHTO 1999, 55).

Driveways

Here we are looking mainly at residential driveways. Driveways for commercial and industrial buildings are more like roads; they get a lot of traffic and may have to support heavy trucks. In contrast, residential driveways need only support cars and light trucks.

Driveways are good candidates for pervious concrete. Modern American houses have enormous driveways, usually paved with impervious concrete or asphalt. Switching to pervious concrete can substantially reduce the percentage of impervious surface on the property and in the neighborhood.

I can't think of any good arguments against pervious concrete for driveways, except the esthetic one. If you are building a fancy house, you might want a fancy driveway, and plain pervious concrete looks, well, plain. It lacks the formality of brick pavers, stone, or stamped dense concrete. That need not be a fatal flaw, however. You can mix pervious concrete with more elegant materials to get the benefits of both.

Parking lots

If pervious concrete were a new electronic gadget, parking lots would be its "killer app". No other application for pervious concrete offers so much promise with so few drawbacks.

Parking lots cover acres and acres, and in many parts of town they form the biggest component of the impervious landscape. Most modern shopping centers and institutions like hospitals consist of buildings surrounded by hundreds or thousands of parked cars, all sitting on impervious asphalt. To meet rules regulating runoff and stormwater control, such projects often need costly features such as underground drains and detention or retention ponds. Switching to pervious concrete in the parking lots can change all that.

This parking lot in Murfreesboro, Tennessee, has drive lanes of dense asphalt and parking stalls of pervious concrete.

This parking lot in Williamsburg, Virginia, is paved almost wholly with pervious concrete.

Objections to pervious concrete for parking usually center on cost, freeze-thaw damage, and snowplowing. When looking at cost, we need to consider the pavement's whole price. As I write this in 2009, a square foot of pervious concrete costs more than a square foot of dense concrete or dense asphalt. That may not always be true in the future. But in any case the cost of the paving material is never the whole price. When you add in curbs, drains, ponds, and water treatment, pervious sometimes lower the parking lot's overall cost.

Freeze-thaw damage is often raised as an argument against pervious concrete in parking lots. We'll look at that contentious issue later. For now it's enough to recognize that the freeze-thaw risk is either negligible or manageable in almost every climate and location.

Some parking-lot designers specify dense concrete or asphalt for the drive aisles, reserving pervious concrete for the parking stalls. Others use pervious concrete all over.

Resistance to snowplow damage is one area where pervious concrete is clearly inferior to dense concrete or dense asphalt. Plow blades catch on its relatively rough surface, tearing aggregate loose. No one has come up with a way to make pervious concrete immune to such damage, though smaller aggregate may help. The only solution is to lift the blade slightly when plowing.

Patios and plazas

These are outdoor pavements used for dining and socializing. Patios are usually connected to private houses or small businesses. Plazas are public, and usually bigger. Both are meant for foot traffic, though some plazas may have to support the occasional motor vehicle.

Patios and plazas are a lot like footpaths, except they are wider and sometimes need to be more decorative. Where plain pervious concrete looks too stark, consider a contrasting border, color, or a stamped pattern.

In dense housing developments, the use of pervious-concrete patios, in place of the more usual dense concrete, can sometimes eliminate the need for detention and retention ponds. Several years ago a developer in my own town, Lexington, built some townhouses with patios of dense concrete. Because the total impervious surface exceeded the code-imposed limit, he dug a detention pond on an adjacent lot. In the end, though, the city denied him the right to that detention pond. To meet the code without the pond, he tore out the concrete patios and replaced them with wood decks. Pervious concrete would have prevented all the expense and trouble.

Sports surfaces

Concrete slabs make good playing surfaces for many games, including basketball, tennis, and volleyball. Dense concrete is usual and generally does the job, but it suffers from one big drawback. Water ponds on it, and nobody wants to play ball games in standing water. The usual preventive for ponding is to slope the pavement, but that creates problems since many games call for a level, or nearly level, playing surface. Some authorities recommend a 1.5% maximum slope for basketball, and 1% for tennis. But for positive drainage the slope should exceed 2% at the very least, and 3% is safer. Something has to give, and it's usually the drainage.

Pervious concrete offers the perfect solution to that dilemma. A ball court made of pervious concrete can be as level as you care to make it, and it will still be ready for play as soon as the rain stops.

One minor drawback to pervious concrete for sports surfaces is that it doesn't take markings as well as smoother materials. Tape won't work. You can paint stripes on it, but the results aren't quite as neat as you get on smooth, dense concrete.

Flatness matters on sports surfaces — far more than it does on driveways and patios. If placing a sports surface in strips, you need to take special care to avoid noticeable bumps and dips at the joints between the strips.

Streets and roads

This is the paving category where doubts about pervious concrete run deepest. Many people who cheerfully accept pervious concrete in parking lots and footpaths balk at using it in public thoroughfares. With only very limited exceptions, government agencies just don't pave streets and roads with pervious materials.

And yet the potential is too great to ignore. All the benefits of pervious concrete apply as strongly to streets and road as to any other kind of pavement.

This city street in Canal Winchester, Ohio, has parking lanes of colored, pervious concrete.

Objections to pervious concrete for streets and roads center on durability and protection of the subgrade. Opponents fear the concrete will ravel under heavy traffic. And they worry about the effect of all that water draining down into the subgrade, weakening it.

Those are reasonable concerns, but they need not prevent pervious concrete's use. A strong mix and good compaction go a long way toward stopping raveling under traffic. The argument for keeping water from the subgrade is stronger. Some soils really do need to be kept as dry as possible. They need impervious pavements on top and that's not going to change. But many soils can take wetting and drying while giving reasonable support.

The day will never come when every road is paved in pervious concrete. But the number of pervious streets and roads will rise from today's low level.

Livestock facilities

Farmers find concrete slabs convenient for many purposes related to raising livestock. But dense concrete has some distinct drawbacks on the farm. Liquid (I hesitate to call it water) collects on top, mixing with solids to make a slippery mess. Runoff is heavily polluted with pathogens, excess nutrients, and suspended particles. Treating the runoff to remove those pollutants is costly and sometimes ineffective.

Though pervious concrete pavements on livestock farms remain rare, the promise is great. Pervious concrete is good at filtering solids from liquids, and that is a key step in managing pollution from livestock. One test poured 10 in. (254 mm) of water through pervious concrete samples that had been covered with cattle manure and bedding. Practically none of the manure and bedding made it through the concrete. Well over 90% remained on top where it could be scraped off. The rest was trapped within the concrete (Luck 2007, 33).

The Kentucky Horse Park near Lexington has built a horse-washing facility with a pervious-concrete floor (Higgins 2007).

Non-pavement uses

Pervious concrete's usefulness is not confined to paving. The material has appeared in drainpipes and walls.

Wall construction was pervious concrete's main application before the 1980s. The oldest reference to no-fines concrete I have seen, from 1951, makes no mention of water passing through. Instead it talks about the concrete's light weight and insulating value, with the idea it could be used in walls (Valore 1951, 833-846). (Actually it's not clear whether the no-fines concrete described in the 1951 article would have been pervious. Made with a massive dose of air-entraining admixture, it may not have contained the connected voids necessary for pervious concrete.)

In the second half of the twentieth century, Europeans build houses and apartment blocks with bearing walls made of cast-in-place pervious concrete. They went as high as eight stories. Since the ability to transmit water is hardly a virtue in a wall, the concrete was covered with stucco on the outside and plaster on the inside.

The chief advantage of pervious concrete in walls is thermal insulation. It's thermal conductivity is only about half that of dense concrete (Murdock 1991, 384).

Chapter 3
Objections and Alternatives

Not everybody likes pervious concrete. And even its strongest supports agree that it's not the right material for every paving job. In this chapter we will look first at some of the general objections that have been raised against pervious concrete. Then we will consider some specific situations in which pervious concrete might not be the wisest choice. Last we will examine other pervious materials for pavements.

General objections

Arguments against pervious concrete almost always raise one or more of these objections:

- It costs too much.
- It ravels under traffic.
- It doesn't look good.
- Frost can damage it.

Cost
Pervious concrete ought to cost less than dense concrete. Roughly one fifth of its volume is free, consisting of air, and you can use ordinary aggregates and cements for the rest.

But it always costs more — sometimes a lot more. The following factors have all been cited as reasons for the higher cost:

- slower concrete placement, due to difficulties in getting pervious concrete out of ready-mix trucks;
- extra hand labor needed to shovel and rake the concrete;
- need for expensive admixtures;
- contractual requirements to use only certified installers.

Those are weak arguments. Though they all contain some truth, even taken together they cannot explain the price differentials often seen between pervious and dense concrete. I suspect that pervious concrete costs more mainly because people are still unfamiliar with it. As its use grows, the cost differential will shrink.

Even at today's prices, pervious concrete doesn't always cost more if you look at the whole job, and not just the concrete slab. On many project switching from impervious to pervious paving materials eliminates the need for curbs, drains, and retention or detention ponds. The savings can be huge, and often fully offset the extra cost of the pervious concrete itself.

Raveling
All pavements experience wear from traffic. On pervious concrete the wear normally takes the form of raveling, in which whole aggregate particles break free.

Severe raveling has occurred where vehicles make sharp turns.

Raveling is a real problem, but the extent to which it forms a valid reason not to use pervious concrete depends on the traffic. The risk is negligible on footpaths and patios, since they need only support people walking around. The risk is large on a busy freeway, where fast truck traffic takes a toll on any paving material. Motor vehicles making tight turns are harder on the pavement surface than the same vehicles driving straight. That's why some parking-lot designers use pervious concrete only in the parking stalls, sticking with dense concrete or dense asphalt in the lanes where cars turn. Snowplowing can ravel any pervious-concrete pavement, unless the blade is lifted slightly so it doesn't scrape.

Though some raveling is probably inevitable and should be considered the normal mode of wear and tear, good design and construction practices can minimize it.

Stronger concrete ravels less. Good, even compaction at the pavement surface also reduces raveling. Some people say that concrete made of angular crushed rock ravels less than that made of rounded gravel. Pervious concrete seems to ravel first at joints. Leaving the joints out and letting slabs crack may reduce the problem.

Even the soundest pavements often ravel a little when they are new.

Looks

The first time I laid eyes on pervious concrete, I was, well, underwhelmed by its appearance. Other people have told me of similar experiences. You think it's going to look like dense concrete with an exposed-aggregate finish. But it doesn't, because the aggregate, though visible in shape, is shrouded in grey cement paste.

I don't mean to say pervious concrete is ugly. Knowing what it can do, I've grown rather fond of its appearance. But it does have a rough, informal look. Sometimes you want that, and other times you don't.

Pervious concrete fits well in rural and natural settings. It looks great in parks and woodlands. It works around suburban houses and commercial properties with informal landscaping.

It looks less appropriate around formal buildings and fancy lawns. Few people would choose unadorned pervious concrete to go in front of a neoclassical courthouse or along an ornate brick wall.

A mix of paving materials give this public market in Boone County, Kentucky, an elegant look that would be impossible with pervious concrete alone.

This street in Canal Winchester, Ohio, achieves a striking look by combining asphalt, unusually bright dense concrete, and colored pervious concrete.

Does that mean pervious concrete is out for formal settings? Not necessarily. Consider these ways to upgrade its appearance:

Surround the pervious concrete with other paving materials. A border of dense concrete, bricks, or cut stone can markedly change a pavement's appearance. Even concrete curbs and gutters, though not needed for drainage, give pervious concrete a more urban look.

Color the concrete. You can do this with a pigment added to the mix, or with a stain applied later.

Apply a stamped finish. This involves pressing a patterned mat into the fresh concrete.

Use smaller aggregate. Some people think pervious concrete looks better when made with pea gravel instead of bigger rocks. There isn't much difference in performance.

Grind the pavement's surface to expose the aggregate. But take care not to clog the concrete with the grinding residue.

If those changes won't give the look you aim for but you still need a pervious pavement, consider pervious block pavers.

Frost damage

This is the number one objection to pervious concrete anywhere winter temperatures regularly fall below freezing. The continuing strength of this objection is surprising, when you consider these three facts:

- Pervious concrete pavements have survived for decades in England without frost damage. Though England is hardly known for brutal winters, it experiences many freeze-thaw cycles and has a wet climate, which makes damage more likely.
- Pervious concrete pavements have survived for years in north-central Pennsylvania and northern Illinois without frost damage. Both areas have cold winters, wet climates, and many freeze-thaw cycles.
- No one can point to a single example of frost damage on a pervious-concrete pavement. Even if the risk is real, it seems that no actual damage has occurred yet, anywhere in the world.

In view of all that, why do people keep raising the specter of frost damage when pervious concrete is proposed? I think there are two explanations.

First, laboratory tests show that freezing can indeed damage pervious concrete, provided the material is full of water when freezing occurs. How often that condition occurs in real life is debatable. But if it does occur, so can frost damage.

Second, it is easy to imagine a set of conditions that would lead to frost damage in the field. Picture a pavement near the end of a long, cold winter. Frost has penetrated the ground several feet deep. The concrete is covered with snow. Along comes a sudden thaw, melting the snow and filling the concrete's pours with water. But the meltwater can't drain away because the subgrade is still frozen. Now the temperature falls well below freezing again, turning the meltwater into ice. The refrozen meltwater is the agent that could destroy the pavement.

If you are with me so far, you have probably already compared my scenario to your home conditions. If you live in Georgia, you know these conditions will never occur where you live. But if you live in Manitoba, they might. Clearly your level of concern for frost damage will depend on your location.

Along those lines, the National Ready Mixed Concrete Association (NRMCA), which generally takes the position that the risk of frost damage is low, divides the American climate into four categories (Freeze 2004, 2-3):

- Dry freeze, where temperatures often fall below freezing and rainfall is low. Much of the western United States falls in this category.
- Wet freeze, where temperatures often fall below freezing and rainfall is high. In the United States much of the South, the Mid-Atlantic States, and the lower Midwest fall in this category.
- Hard dry freeze, where temperatures stay below freezing for long periods and rainfall is low. This occurs in the western United States at high elevations.
- Hard wet freeze, where temperatures stay below freezing for long periods and rainfall is high. The upper Midwest, parts of New England, and much of Canada fall in this category.

The risk of frost damage is low in the first three categories. Freezing will occur, but the concrete is highly unlikely to be saturated at the time. Only the hard wet freeze category puts pervious concrete at serious risk. In that climate, and only in that climate, the NRMCA recommends one or more of these defenses (Freeze 2004, 2-3):

- an aggregate sub-base 8-24 in. (200-600 mm) thick;
- perforated pipes to drain the sub-base;
- an air-entraining admixture in the concrete mix.

Up to now we have been talking about just one kind of frost damage, the sort that happens after the concrete has set. Frost can also damage fresh concrete before it has set. But the risk for that is the same for pervious and impervious concretes, and it's easy to avoid. Just don't place concrete if it could freeze during its first 24 hours.

Where not to use pervious concrete

Even supporters of pervious concrete agree there are some places where it should not be used, or should be used only with caution. Those places include:

- brownfield sites;
- steep slopes;
- sites with expansive clay soil.

What these locations have in common is the likelihood of problems if too much water enters the ground.

Brownfield sites are old industrial properties that are being redeveloped for some new purpose. The ground in these sites is often contaminated. Building a pervious pavement over contaminated soil can cause trouble, especially where the ground cover used to be impervious. Stormwater that formerly ran off can now penetrate the ground, where it can flush out pollutants and carry them downstream.

Steep slopes cause trouble because water penetrating the concrete can wash out the subgrade, undermining the pavement. Ferguson says problems can occur where the slope exceeds 5% (2005, 59). He may be too conservative, however. Pervious concrete has been used successfully on much steeper slopes.

Expansive clay is soil that expands greatly when it gets wet, and shrinks greatly as it dries out. It is hard to make any pavement work over expansive clay, especially where the climate includes distinct wet and dry seasons. Pervious pavement complicates the problem by flooding the subgrade with water after every rain. And to make the situation even worse, some of the design details that help pavements succeed on expansive clay — post-tensioning, heavy reinforcement, and piling — are not practical with pervious concrete.

You can use pervious concrete on some problem sites by putting a liner under it and draining off the water that passes through the slab. You then lose most of the stormwater-control benefits. But you still get a reduction in ponding.

Pervious alternatives

Concrete is far from the only option when you want a pervious pavement. Here are the chief alternatives:

- pervious asphalt;
- pervious block pavers;
- turf;
- grass grids;
- unbound aggregate;
- mulch.

Pervious asphalt

This consists of open-graded coarse aggregate bound with asphalt, a tar-like resin made from petroleum. It is a close substitute for pervious concrete, with practically the same ability to infiltrate water. Many goals you might wish to accomplish with pervious concrete can be met about as well with pervious asphalt. The rivalry between the two pervious materials replicates the long competition between dense asphalt and dense concrete for the regular, impervious pavement market. Asphalt and concrete have been duking it out there for over a century, so don't expect a resolution tomorrow.

Pervious asphalt looks and acts a lot like pervious concrete. This asphalt parking lot is in Georgetown, Kentucky.

These pervious block pavers cover a heavily-used parking lot at the Morton Arboretum in Lisle, Illinois.

Pervious asphalt and pervious concrete are not quite interchangeable, however. One big difference lies in how they interact with their bases. (Asphalt people use the term base to describe the aggregate layer under the wearing course. Concrete people call it a sub-base.) Asphalt bends easily, so it needs a firm base. Concrete is stiff, so it can tolerate a weaker base. Highway engineers recognize this as the key difference between asphalt and concrete roads, calling the former flexible pavements and the latter rigid pavements. The difference in base requirements applies to pervious and impervious pavements alike. But the distinction is sharper with pervious pavements, because you can only go so far in stabilizing a base before you render it impervious.

There has been some use of pervious asphalt on roads as a topping — called a friction course — over a pavement that is otherwise impervious. That reduces ponding but doesn't control stormwater.

Some pervious asphalt pavements have suffered from draindown. This occurs during construction when the hot binder drips off the aggregate. The result is a weak surface that ravels under traffic, and sometimes a bottom layer that is sealed and impervious. Draindown can affect pervious concrete, too.

Some people object to pervious asphalt on environmental grounds, saying that as it breaks down it releases petrochemicals.

Pervious block pavers

Block pavers are masonry units about as big as common bricks, laid without mortar over an aggregate base. Some are real bricks made of burnt clay. Most are made of ordinary dense concrete, often colored. Cut stone is also an option.

You can't use any old blocks to make a pervious pavement, however. Ordinary pavers fit together tightly, and the narrow gaps between blocks are filled with fine sand. A pavement made like that is only slightly more pervious than dense concrete or asphalt. In contrast, pavers meant for pervious work are made to fit together with wider gaps, or else the pavers themselves contain holes. The gaps and holes are filled with coarse sand or fine gravel.

A rough and ready way to make a pervious block pavement is to use ordinary building bricks that have holes in them. Though the holes weren't put there to make the bricks pervious, they work for that purpose when filled with coarse sand. But don't try this in an area of heavy traffic, because common bricks don't resist abrasion well.

Block pavers lean toward a distinctive, formal look. They can provide a pleasing visual contrast to asphalt or cast-in-place concrete. They look good in locations where pervious concrete might appear too rough or rustic. Since they are easy to remove and replace, they make a good choice for a pavement that may need to be taken up now and then for access to underground utilities.

Though not suitable for high-speed travel, block pavements serve well for parking lots and driveways. They can be designed to support heavy vehicles, including fully loaded highway trucks. Cyclists dislike them, however. And they can be tricky for pedestrians wearing high heels.

Ordinary building bricks with holes have been used for pervious paving.

Unbound aggregate has higher permeability than any other paving material, though pervious concrete comes close.

Turf

If you drove your car across your lawn every day, you wouldn't have much of a lawn. But if you pulled your car onto the grass now and then for a washing, no harm would come of it. Though useless for daily traffic or daily parking, turf can serve well for occasional overflow parking or for special events.

Surprisingly, turf is markedly worse than pervious concrete at taking in water, though it still beats dense concrete and asphalt by a mile. Infiltration rates for turf range from 0.2 to 3.9 in./hr (5 to 99 mm.hr), while runoff coefficients range from 0.05 to 0.53 (Ferguson, 124-126).

Though literally green, turf isn't always as green (in the sense of promoting sustainability and protecting the environment) as it might seem. It requires mowing, and some people dump a lot of fertilizer and pesticides on it. In many climates it needs irrigation to stay healthy.

Where turf excels is in the mitigation of heat islands. Like all green plants, it constantly pumps water out of the ground and releases it into the air — a process called transpiration. This natural cooling system keeps turf cooler on sunny days than concrete or asphalt.

Grass grids

These are strong mats that distribute vehicle loads, while leaving plenty of holes for grass to grow through. A grass-grid pavement looks like turf from a distance, but can support heavier and more frequent traffic.

Grass grids are sometimes used for daily parking, but are more common in areas where cars are parked only occasionally.

Unbound aggregate

This is loose rock particles, without cement or asphalt to lock them in place. If you dump a load of gravel so you can drive through a muddy spot, you're paving with unbound aggregate.

The aggregate must be open-graded with nothing smaller than about 3/8 inch (10 mm). Gradations suitable for making pervious concrete generally serve for unbound aggregate. Indeed, you can view it as pervious concrete without the cement. You should avoid rounded shapes, however, because they roll like ball bearings under traffic. Crushed rock usually works better than natural gravel.

Under no circumstances should you use all-in aggregates that contain a blend of coarse and fine particles. Such products go by different names — crusher-run, ABC stone, roadbase. Because they contain fines, they pack tightly under traffic and become impervious.

Unbound aggregate can take very heavy loads, including big trucks, if you put it down thick enough. It's also suitable for pedestrian traffic, though it doesn't always make for the most pleasant walking. Cyclists generally don't like it, and it won't work for handicapped access.

Unbound aggregate requires frequent maintenance, but the maintenance is easy, consisting mainly of grading and occasionally adding more rock. It doesn't wear out or break down as concrete and asphalt pavements do. It fails by being displaced horizontally, and by being driven down into the subgrade so that it more or less disappears.

Mulch

This is a bed of loose, soft particles. Mulch resembles unbound aggregate, except that mulch particles are soft and usually of organic origin. Most mulches come from plants. Examples include wood chips, bark chips, shredded bark, and chopped up sticks and brush. However, one non-plant-based material has appeared in recent years: chopped rubber from recycled tires. That's a source not likely to run short anytime soon.

People don't often think of mulch as a paving material. Its main uses are to protect plant roots and beautify gardens. But it makes an effective surface for foot traffic and the occasional motor vehicle. And it's hard to imagine a greener pavement. You can make it out of local materials and place it with hand tools.

Mulch can't support heavy loads, so it's generally not a good choice for driveways and parking lots. It's best limited to foot traffic, with the occasional maintenance vehicle and perhaps a few bicycles. It is not suitable for handicapped access.

Mulch pavements find their widest use in parks. They make attractive, comfortable footpaths that blend well with woodlands and grass. And parks can often make their own mulch cheaply, grinding up plant debris from deadfalls and ice storms.

Given equal traffic, mulch needs more maintenance than unbound aggregate. In addition to being displaced by traffic, mulches — at least the plant-based ones — gradually rot and return to the soil as humus. But the maintenance is simple. Just add more mulch.

Mulch makes an attractive paving material for lightly-used footpaths.

Chapter 4
Designing the Pavement

The design of a pervious-concrete pavement involves two big steps and several smaller ones. The big steps are hydrologic design and structural design. Hydrologic design deals with water and how a pavement handles it. Structural design deals with loads and how a pavement supports them. The smaller steps include decisions on the concrete mix and joints.

Hydrologic design

This can be simple or complex.

Simple designs aim only to minimize the effect on water's natural flow. If you don't overcompact the subgrade and ensure that the new pavement contains no impervious layers, the results are likely to satisfy. This approach makes sense for small projects like sidewalks and driveways. And it sometimes works for much bigger projects, in areas where stormwater is not strictly regulated.

Complex designs require detailed analysis of how water enters the pavement, how long it stays there, and how it leaves. The process requires weather data and, often, soil testing to determine the infiltration rate.

While I would never try to discourage anyone from undertaking a detailed analysis of any pavement, we should recognize the limitations of the complex approach. Two key numbers, the maximum rainfall rate and the infiltration rate of the native soil, are estimates at best and wild guesses at worst. The first is a matter of weather. And though weather is amenable to statistical analysis, it does not lend itself to precise predictions. On top of that, weather data are only available for certain spots. Unless you are building next door to the weather station, you can't be sure the statistics apply to your site. The second key number, the soil's infiltration rate, can indeed be measured precisely, but it changes with the seasons and with moisture levels. The infiltration rate on the day of the heaviest rainfall could be a lot lower than on the day you made your tests.

Because of those uncertainties, hydrologic design of pervious pavements will always be less precise than, say,

the design of a steel bridge beam to support a locomotive. And that's OK. If you get the bridge beam wrong, the train crashes and people die. If you get the pervious pavement wrong, the results will be, at worst, some unwanted runoff. Even then the runoff will surely be less than an impervious pavement would have allowed.

The hydrologic design process

A full hydrologic design typically involves these steps:

1. Decide on the goals.

2. Examine the inputs. Find out how much water will reach the pavement in the most severe weather event you want to design for.

3. Determine the site's infiltration rate. How fast will water soak into the native soil?

4. Compare the input to the infiltration rate to see whether the pavement needs a reservoir.

5. If a reservoir is needed, calculate its required capacity.

6. Come up with an economic combination of slab and sub-base to provide the required reservoir capacity.

7. If it proves impractical to provide enough reservoir capacity, or if the drawdown time is too long, specify an alternative drainage method.

Goals

Before undertaking a detailed hydrologic design, decide what you expect the pavement to accomplish. On many jobs the goal is zero runoff, with practically all water captured on site and slowly infiltrated into the ground. On other jobs runoff is expected, but you want to reduce its volume or improve its quality. And some jobs call for water to be harvested for use after it passes through the pavement.

Inputs

Water enters a pavement from two sources. It falls directly on the pavement in the form of rain and snow.

Here a narrow strip of pervious concrete is expected to take in water from a much bigger asphalt pavement. This is a library parking lot in Powell, Tennessee.

It also flows onto the pavement from nearby surfaces. In some cases there may be other sources such as irrigation sprinklers or the washing of vehicles, but they rarely control the design.

Inputs are expressed as the depth of liquid water in inches or millimeters. For rain, this is what you would get if you left an open pan outside and measured the depth of the water that accumulates in it during a storm. (The pan's sides have to be vertical, and we are assuming that none of the water evaporates).

Rainfall is easy to measure. Deciding how much rainfall to design for is hard. Some people start out thinking they will allow for the worst possible case, but that's impossible to predict. Instead, you work with a design rain event calculated from weather statistics. Picking the design rain

event requires two decisions. First, you have to choose the event's length. Some designers consider the rainfall over 24 hours, but that period may be too short in some climates. Second, you have to choose the return period.

Everybody has run into the concept of return periods from discussions of flooding, where it's usual to talk about 100-year and 500-year events. But many people misunderstand the terms. Here is the explanation I find simplest: the probability of the event's occurring in any one year is the reciprocal of the return period. Thus there is a 1/100 or 1% probability that the 100-year flood will take place this year.

But in pervious-pavement design the return periods are always far shorter than those used to predict major floods. Many designers choose a two-year period. This means that several storms exceeding the design rain event will almost certainly occur over the pavement's lifespan.

Let's suppose the weather records show the 24-hour, two-year rain event to be 3.2 in. (81 mm). That means in any given year there is a 50% probability that 3.2 in. (81 mm) of rain, or more, will fall in a 24-hour period.

In addition to determining the size of the design rain event, some designers also look at the maximum rainfall expected per hour. That's like using a 1-hour event length. Such information can be useful because the infiltration rate for each pavement layer is normally expressed in inches or millimeters per hour. Whenever the rainfall rate exceeds the infiltration rate, water will pond on or run off that layer.

Infiltration

Water leaves a site in three main ways. It sinks into the ground in a process called infiltration. It runs off on the surface. And it drains away in artificial devices such as pipes and trenches. In addition, some water leaves by evaporation and is taken up by plant roots, but those routes are rarely considered in hydrologic design.

Infiltration is generally what you want, so you need to know the ground's infiltration rate, also called its permeability. This is expressed as the depth of liquid water infiltrated in an hour. The usual units are inches per hour or millimeters per hour. ASTM offers three tests for infiltration: ASTM D 2434, ASTM D 3385, and ASTM D 5093.

Infiltration rates range from close to zero on solid rock or dense concrete, to as much as 100 in./hr on loose gravel. The table below shows typical values for various soils, all of which are assumed to be only lightly compacted:

Infiltration rates in lightly compacted soils (Ferguson 2005, 144)

Surface	Infiltration rate (in./hr)	Infiltration rate (mm/hr)
Sand	8.27	210
Loamy sand	2.41	61
Sandy loam	1.02	26
Loam	0.52	13
Silty loam	0.27	6.9
Sandy clay loam	0.17	4.3
Clay loam	0.09	2.3
Silty clay loam	0.06	1.5
Sandy clay	0.05	1.3
Silty clay	0.04	1.0
Clay	0.02	0.5

To put those numbers in perspective, consider that natural forest soils can take in 8 to 60 in/hr (200 to 1500 mm/hr), while established turf on undisturbed soil absorbs 1.9 to 3.9 in/hr (48 to 99 mm/hr) (Ferguson 2005, 124).

Pervious concrete infiltrates water faster than almost any natural surface. For that reason the infiltration rate of the concrete never controls the hydrologic design. The limiting factor in how water enters the ground almost always lies in the subgrade, and not in the slab or sub-base.

Water entering this parking lot in Williamsburg, Virginia, is harvested to irrigate the ornamental plants nearby.

One guidebook suggests that soil with an infiltration rate above 1/2 in./hr (12mm/hr) is generally suitable for use with pervious concrete, and that soil measuring below that value will sometimes work (Tennis 2004, 13).

You would think that as long as the infiltration rate exceeds the rainfall rate, no water would run off. That's not quite true, however, because infiltration rates are measured under conditions that do not duplicate normal rainfall. In real life even highly pervious surfaces produce some runoff. The likelihood of this is expressed as the surface's runoff coefficient: the volume of runoff divided by the volume of rainfall. Runoff coefficients range from 0 (nothing running off) to 1 (everything running off).

Though infiltration is usually desirable, there are a few situations in which it is not. You might not want to allow for infiltration into the ground if your site includes any of the following:

- contaminated soil;
- steep slopes;
- expansive clay soil.

To prevent infiltration, put a liner over the subgrade. But you then have to drain the water off another way, and will lose much of the stormwater-control benefits.

Reservoir capacity

If the ground's infiltration rate is greater than the expected input rate during the design rain event, you don't need a reservoir. You need only make sure the pavement's own infiltration rate is high enough, and that's easy. Pervious concrete, if properly built and maintained, has an infiltration rate of 670 to 900 in/hr. You'd have to build under a waterfall to find inputs that high.

You won't always find soils that are pervious enough, however. Most natural soils can't infiltrate water as fast as it arrives in the design rain event. They need reservoirs to store that water.

Reservoir capacity is measured in inches or millimeters, showing the depth of water that can be stored. The required capacity is the depth of water supplied in the design rain event, minus any amount that soaks into the subgrade or flows out in drains during the event.

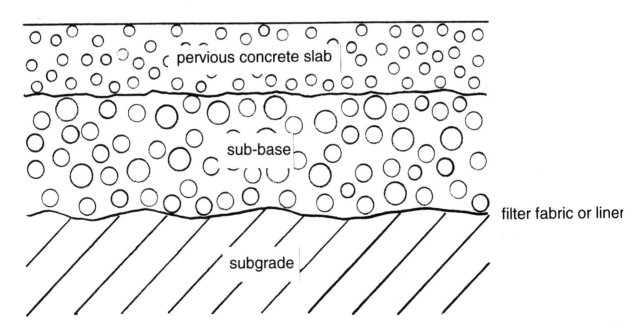

Every pervious-concrete pavement includes a slab and a subgrade. The other components are optional.

The reservoir normally consists of the void space in the concrete slab and in the sub-base. If the pavement is level, calculate reservoir capacity from the following equations:

$$r = [(h_{slab})(v_{slab}) + (h_{base})(v_{base})] / 100$$

Where
r = reservoir capacity
h_{slab} = thickness of pervious concrete slab
v_{slab} = percentage of voids in pervious concrete slab
h_{base} = thickness of granular sub-base
v_{base} = percentage of voids in sub-base

The values for r, h_{slab}, and h_{base} can be in any units, as long as you stick to the same units for all three.

Designers often assume a 20% void content for pervious concrete. But you should use another value if you have good reason to believe it's closer to the truth. Nowadays some people aim for a void content as low as 16 or 17%, though that's hard to reach. If you are trying to make concrete with 16% voids, that's the number to use when calculating reservoir capacity.

Sub-bases, if made of open-graded coarse aggregate, have void contents of about 40%. Since sub-base materials normally have higher void contents than even the most porous of pervious concretes, and cost less to boot, it's wise to use the sub-base for as much of the reservoir as you can without degrading the structural design.

The full thickness of slab and sub-base is only available where the pavement is level. With sloped pavements water collects at the downhill end. If the slope is slight and the pavement small, you can just make do with the reduced reservoir capacity. If the slope or pavement size is great, special measures may be needed to get a big enough reservoir. One option is to terrace the sub-grade so that the bottom of the reservoir consists of a series of steps. Another option is to dig trenches in the subgrade at right angles to the slope.

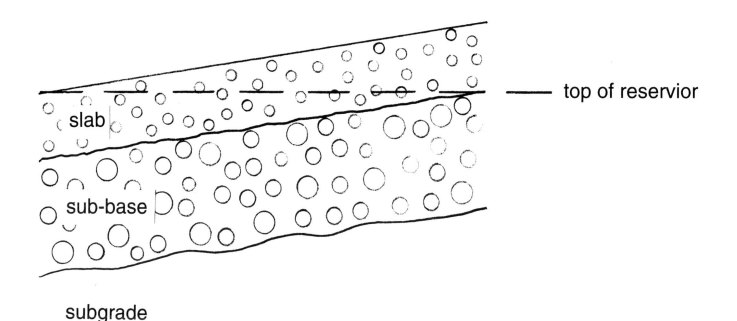

When a pavement slopes, the full depth of slab and sub-base is not available as a reservoir.

Light-duty slabs are often 4 in. (100 mm) thick.

Some designers prefer not to use the concrete slab as part of the reservoir. They rely solely on the sub-base, which must then be thick enough to hold all the water.

In some cases it may be impractical to provide a reservoir big enough for the design rain event. This happens most often on sloped sites or where the pervious pavement takes in a lot of runoff from adjacent surfaces. The simplest solution is just to accept that the pavement will overflow in some storms. In effect, you are then designing for a lesser rain event. If that's not acceptable, the usual remedy is to carry some of the water off in underslab drains — typically through perforated pipes.

Drawdown time

It's not enough for the reservoir to take in all the water from the design rain event. The water needs to drain out before the next storm comes along. The time needed for a full reservoir to empty is called the drawdown time. To calculate it, divide the reservoir capacity by the subgrade's infiltration rate.

If drawdown will take longer than five days, you have a problem. To reduce it, either increase the infiltration rate or drain the reservoir another way.

On some sites you can increase infiltration by digging out and replacing the most troublesome layer. Other options include trenches or dry wells.

Where infiltration just won't do the job, you can drain some of the water off through pipes or aggregate-filled trenches under the slab. But then you have to put that water somewhere, and that leads to solutions such as detention ponds that you had probably hoped to avoid by switching to pervious concrete.

Structural design

While hydrologic design aims to ensure the pavement can handle water, structural design aims to ensure the pavement can handle loads. The principles of structural design apply equally to pervious and impervious pavements.

Most designers use one of the standard design methods meant for unreinforced rigid pavements, even though the creators of those methods may not have given pervious concrete a moment's thought. The American Concrete Institute publishes a guide for parking lots (ACI 330R, 2003). Several methods, including proprietary computer programs, are available for designing concrete streets and roads.

While pervious concrete slabs are usually considered to be rigid pavements for purposes of structural design, it may also be possible to design them along the lines of flexible pavements (Tennis 2004, 15).

Full-blown structural analysis is generally reserved for parking lots, roads, and streets. Few designers bother with calculations for lightly loaded pavements such as sidewalks, patios, and sports surfaces. Such slabs are normally 4 in. (100 mm) thick, unless hydrologic design calls for more.

Subgrade

The standard design methods all rely on some value for the subgrade's ability to support loads. That ability is often expressed as the modulus of subgrade reaction (also called subgrade modulus or K-value), or the California bearing ratio (abbreviated CBR). Both are measures of how much the subgrade deforms when a load is placed on it.

You can measure subgrade modulus with a plate-bearing test, or you can assume it from the type of soil found on site. Either way, the right value to use in the design may differ from what you would use for an impervious pavement. There are two reasons for that: compaction and moisture content.

Compaction improves the subgrade modulus, and that's why ordinary pavement designs assume the ground will be reasonably well compacted. That's an assumption we should not make in designing a pervious pavement. Compaction reduces the subgrade's infiltration rate, so we have to use it cautiously. Some compaction of the subgrade may be necessary, and some occurs inadvertently from construction traffic, but you don't want to overdo it.

Moisture content comes into play because pervious pavements, by design, result in a soaked subgrade after every heavy rain. In contrast, traditional impervious pavements, both concrete and asphalt, shield the ground from rainfall and reduce moisture changes in the subgrade. Some designers of impervious pavements go to considerable lengths to keep the subgrade dry, calling for the sealing of all joints and cracks.

When analyzing the subgrade for a pervious pavement, assume it will not be well compacted and will sometimes be soaked with water. You may have to use a lower subgrade modulus or CBR than the geotechnical engineer's first estimate.

Reinforcement

Pervious concrete never (well, almost never) contains reinforcement. Reinforcing steel would not bond well and would be vulnerable to corrosion. Structural design must be based on the principles of unreinforced concrete.

Concrete mix design

Nowadays concrete mix designs usually come from the ready-mix concrete supplier. Pavement designers aren't expected to be experts in mix design. But they do need to know what to ask for. Specifications often cover:

- void content;
- concrete strength;
- aggregate type and gradation;
- air entrainment.

Void content matters for hydrologic design, and concrete strength matters for structural design. Regrettably, the two properties are inversely correlated. If your design needs both high void content and high strength, you are out of luck. Some people talk about a so-called 25-25 mix design as a reasonable, achievable compromise. That's concrete with 25% voids and 2500-psi compressive strength. (In metric units that would be 25% voids and 17-MPa compressive strength, but a 25-17 mix doesn't have quite the same ring.)

Aggregate type and gradation affect the concrete's appearance, and maybe its tendency to ravel. Many people find that smaller, rounded particles make for a better-looking pavement, though I happen to think big rocks look just fine. On the other hand, you hear stories (no hard test results, though) that angular aggregates ravel less under traffic. In any case, the ability to choose aggregates is limited by what the local supplier has to sell, unless you want to pay extra to truck in something special.

Should you specify entrained air? Opinions vary. Advocates claim it lowers the risk of frost damage, as it unquestionably does for dense concrete. Opponents say pervious concrete is already protected from frost by its low water-cement ratio and free drainage. You'll have to make up your own mind, but the odds for success are good either way. If you live in the tropics you can ignore all this, of course.

Joints and crack control

Concrete wants to crack. Left to its own devices, almost any concrete slab more than a few feet long will crack in response to stresses caused by drying shrinkage and thermal contraction. To control those cracks, we use joints to divide the slab into smaller panels. If the joints are close enough and work as they should, these smaller panels will not crack.

Designers of dense-concrete slabs have other options — reinforcement and prestressing — for crack control. Those options aren't available for pervious concrete.

The choice then comes down to joints versus cracks. We either joint the slab to control cracks, or we let the slab crack on its own. It's not much of a contest where dense-

The shallow sawcut is meant to induce a crack, but this slab hasn't cracked yet.

concrete slabs are concerned. Almost everybody puts in joints, for these reasons:

> Joints look neater than cracks.
> Joints are easier to seal than cracks.
> Joints are traditional.

But those arguments are for joints in dense concrete. They lose much of their force when we apply them to pervious concrete. Many people find that cracks in pervious concrete just don't look that bad. They seldom open wide, and many of them disappear, more or less, into the concrete's naturally rough texture. Sealing is a complete non-issue in pervious concrete. Why would you seal a joint or crack in a slab that's supposed to leak water anyway? As for tradition, I would argue that pervious concrete hasn't been used widely long enough to have much of a tradition.

You can probably tell by now that I'm in the let-it-crack camp. But it can be a tough call. And if you choose to joint your pervious-concrete slab, you then face another hard issue: the distance between joints.

Joint spacing

An old standard rule for dense-concrete slabs says the joint spacing, measured in feet, should not exceed two to three times the slab thickness, measured in inches. Or to say it in a way that makes sense to people who don't work in feet and inches, the joint spacing should not exceed 24 to 36 times the slab thickness. For a slab 4 in. (100 mm) thick, the maximum joint spacing would be between 8 and 12 ft (2.4 and 3.6 m). The lower limit applies where drying shrinkage is expected to be high. The upper limit applies where drying shrinkage is well controlled.

Since pervious concrete shrinks only about half as much as dense concrete and rarely curls noticeably, we should be safe going to the upper end of the joint-spacing range. That would mean joints up to 12 ft (3.6 m) apart in a 4-in. (100-mm) slab. But some designers go well beyond that. Joints in 4-in. (100-mm) pervious slabs are often spaced 16 to 20 ft (5 to 6 m) apart.

Remember, though, that joint spacing remains an inexact science, in pervious and impervious slabs alike. Cracks can occur with any spacing. Almost the only definite statement you can make on the subject is to say that when you reduce the joint spacing you lower the likelihood of cracks. If your tolerance for cracks is low, add more joints.

Making the joints

Unlike the joint spacing, the joint's method of construction doesn't seem to have much effect on crack control. The choice between formed, insert, rolled, and sawn joints comes down to convenience and appearance.

Isolation and expansion joints

The joints we have been talking about up to now lie within the slab and are meant to divide it into small panels for crack control. Such joints are often called control joints, crack-control joints, or contraction joints. Some pavements contain other types of joints, too.

Isolation joints separate the pervious-concrete pavement from other pavements or other structures. Their main purpose is to allow differential settlement without putting undue stress on the slab. They are often used where the concrete slab abuts a wall or curb. Less often, they appear between a pervious-concrete slab and another paving material such as asphalt or dense concrete.

Expansion joints leave room for a pavement slab to expand without putting undue stress on adjacent slabs or other structures. Few pervious-concrete slabs need expansion joints, because they are unlikely ever to expand much beyond their original, as-cast dimensions. However, exceptions exist for long slabs cast in cool weather. On a hot summer day such slabs may expand enough to cause a problem.

Isolation and expansion joints are made in the same way, by casting the concrete against a sheet of compressible material. The material goes by several names: joint filler, filler board, and expansion strip. The material is usually about 1/2 in. (12 mm) thick.

Load transfer at joints

Dense-concrete pavements that get heavy traffic often contain devices to transfer load across the joints. The most common load-transfer devices are steel dowels made of smooth bar stock and tie bars of regular reinforcing steel cut to short lengths. The load transfer devices reduce stress at the slab edge and limit differential movement across the joint.

Pervious-concrete pavements almost never contain dowels or tie bars. They rely instead on aggregate interlock. The idea is that when one side of the joint is pushed down by a load, it can only go a very short distance before its aggregate particles bump into aggregate particles on the joint's other side.

Though aggregate interlock has a dubious reputation in the dense-concrete field, it seems to work pretty well in pervious concrete. Problems related to lack of load transfer have been rare.

That could change, however, as pervious concrete sees more use in heavily loaded pavements like truck parking lots and roads. Research is needed to see whether the load-transfer devices used in dense concrete can be adapted for pervious paving.

Some designers put isolation joints between pervious concrete and other paving materials. The designer here didn't bother, and it turned out fine. This is at the Indiana State Fairground in Indianapolis.

Chapter 5
Making Pervious Concrete

Any of these coarse aggregates can make good pervious concrete. Clockwise from top left, they are:
3/4-in. (20-mm) crushed rock, 3/4-in. (20-mm) natural gravel, and 3/8-in. (10-mm) crushed rock.

Components

Pervious concrete has three essential ingredients and several optional ones. It always contains coarse aggregate, cement, and water. It may or may not contain fine aggregate, pozzolans, admixtures, and fibers.

Coarse aggregate

Aggregate gradations are described as close or open. Close-graded aggregates have a wide range of particle sizes, with substantial amounts retained on several standard sieves. Open-graded aggregates have a narrow range of particle sizes, with most material retained on one or two sieves. Open gradation reaches its extreme with single-size aggregate, in which practically everything is retained on a single sieve.

Consisting predominantly of rock particles at least 3/16 in. (5 mm) across, coarse aggregate makes up the bulk of any pervious-concrete mix. To start with, the coarse aggregate should meet the usual standards for aggregates used in concrete. In the United States it should satisfy ASTM C 33. Coarse aggregate from a concrete supplier normally meets the standard, but aggregate sold for sub-bases or landscaping may not. Beyond that, we need to consider the size and shape of the rock particles.

Aggregate size is determined by passing the material through a series of ever finer sieves and measuring the mass retained on each sieve. The process is called sieve analysis, and the result, gradation.

Pervious concrete requires open-graded coarse aggregate. In contrast, dense concrete turns out better with close-graded aggregate. All else being equal, the closer you get to single-size gradation, the greater the void content will be.

Early guides to pervious concrete recommended single-size aggregate — either 3/8 in. (10 mm) or 3/4 in. (20 mm). That's still a good choice, but it can be hard to find. Recent years have seen increasing use of open-graded aggregates that aren't quite single-size — probably because concrete suppliers already have them on hand for other purposes.

Whatever the reason for the change, open gradations such as #67, #8, and #89 have proven successful in pervious-concrete pavements (Tennis 2004, 7).

The gradation numbers come from ASTM C 33 (2008, 14). The table below shows the size limits for those common gradations:

Size number	Amount passing each sieve (percent by mass)						
	1 in.	3/4 in.	1/2 in.	3/8 in.	No. 4	No. 8	No. 16
67	100	90-100	—	20-55	0-10	0-5	—
8	100	100	100	85-100	10-30	0-10	0-5
89	100	100	100	90-100	20-55	5-30	0-10

While everyone agrees on the need for open gradation, opinions vary widely on exactly what particle size works best. Bigger rocks provide more permeability, but any size that qualifies as coarse is permeable enough, so arguments center on other issues. Some people favor the small end of the range, arguing that concrete made with smaller rocks looks better and achieves higher strength. On the other hand, bigger rocks reduce the risk of sealing and require less cement paste to coat every particle.

Particle shape also matters, and here the choice comes down to angular versus rounded. Angular particles are normally found in crushed rock, while rounded particles are characteristic of natural gravel. Most observers seem to prefer the look of rounded aggregates, and one study shows that rounded pea gravel was better than other aggregates at retaining solid material on the slab surface (Luck 2007, 26). On the other hand, some people say concrete with angular particles ravels less under traffic.

In the end the coarse aggregate is, alas, determined more by supply than by demand. You can ask for anything, but unless you are prepared to pay more — and it can be a lot more — you have to buy what's available in your local market. Fortunately you can make good pervious concrete with a wide range of particle sizes and shapes.

Cement

The binder in pervious concrete is almost always ordinary Portland cement. In the United States, that means Type I or Type II cement. It's made by heating a mixture of limestone and clay till it partially melts, letting it cool, and grinding the result into a fine, grey powder.

White Portland cement might be worth a look if you are desperate for a light-colored, highly reflective pavement. It costs far more than ordinary Portland, however.

Other cements, including Type III for rapid strength gain, Type IV for low heat generation, and Type V for sulfate resistance have little or no place in pervious concrete. In particular you want to stay clear of Type III under normal circumstances. It makes concrete set faster, and that's a change you almost never want with pervious concrete, which sets fast anyway.

Water

Pervious concrete has no special requirements when it comes to the quality of the mixing water. Any water used for dense concrete will serve as well for pervious. The general rule is that if you can drink it, you can make concrete from it, but in truth some non-potable water will work. Though I have not heard of pervious concrete being made with seawater, there is no good argument against it.

While the water's quality is seldom an issue, its quantity always is. Getting the water content right is essential to the success of any pervious-concrete pour. We'll look at that later.

Fine aggregate

This consists of rock particles less than 3/16 in. (5 mm) across. It comes from two sources: natural sand mined from

In the United States, Portland cement comes in a standard bag that weighs 94 lb and holds 1 cu ft.

the earth, and manufactured sand made by crushing rock and sieving out the bigger chunks.

Years ago pervious concrete never contained fine aggregate. Indeed it often went by the name no-fines concrete. You can still make pervious concrete that way, and some people do.

Nowadays, however, if you order pervious concrete from a ready-mix supplier it is likely to contain a little sand. The amount of fine aggregate typically ranges from 50 to 150 lb/cu yd (from 30 to 90 kg/cu m). That's far less than the amount found in dense concrete.

Adding fine aggregate has good and bad effects. The good effects are higher strength and less risk of draindown. The chief bad effect is reduced permeability (Schaefer 2006, 34).

Though the addition of fine aggregate has become common in pervious concrete supplied by ready-mix plants, I would be wary of it when mixing on site. Site-mixed concrete is typically made in much smaller batches than ready-mix. The quantity of fine aggregate then becomes so small it is hard to batch accurately.

Pozzolans

These are powders that have cement-like properties when used with Portland cement. Since they allow a reduction in the amount of cement, pozzolans are also known as cement replacement materials.

The most common pozzolans are fly ash and slag, and both are industrial by-products. Fly ash comes from the smoke emitted by coal-fired power plants. Slag, also called ground granulated blast furnace slab or GGBS, comes from steel-mill waste. Fly ash and slag work similarly, affecting concrete in these ways:

- lower financial cost (usually);
- lower environmental cost;
- longer setting time;
- slower rate of strength gain.

The environmental benefits of fly ash and slag come from their status as industrial by-products, and from the fact that they reduce demand for Portland cement, the most energy-intensive component of pervious concrete.

Because slag makes concrete lighter in color, it is worth considering where reflectivity matters. Designers sometimes specify a surface reflectivity index (SRI) of at least 29 because that qualifies for LEED points. Pervious concrete made with straight Portland cement doesn't reliably meet that requirement, but concrete made with slag usually measures above 29. You can't count on fly ash for the same brightening, though. Some fly ashes (not all) have the opposite effect.

Despite the benefits of pozzolans, you can never replace all the cement with them. Replacement levels for fly ash go up to 30% or so. For slag they go up to 50%. A 30% replacement rate means that 30% of the total cementitious material is pozzolan, and 70% Portland cement.

Admixtures

These are chemicals added to the concrete mix to change its behavior. Admixtures in concrete are like drugs in the human body. They aren't always needed; they work in small doses; and they have side effects.

The admixtures often used in pervious concrete fall into these categories:

air entrainers;
water reducers;
viscosity modifiers;
retarders;
set stabilizers.

Air entrainers introduce small bubbles into the cement paste. The bubbles are spherical with a diameter of 0.0008 to 0.02 in. (0.02 to 0.5 mm). The goal is to improve frost resistance by providing air space that relieves the pressure caused by growing ice crystals.

The use of air entrainers in pervious concrete is controversial. Some authorities recommend them, but a few others stridently oppose them. The most common view seems to be that air entrainers aren't absolutely necessary, but don't cost much and are worth using as extra insurance against frost damage. One issue with air entrainers is the lack of any practical way to determine how well they are working. The usual tests for air content, commonly performed on dense concrete during the pour, don't work on pervious concrete.

Plasticizers make fresh concrete more workable. They are often used in dense concrete to allow a reduction in water content, a practice that explains their other name, water reducers. That name doesn't fit the way plasticizers work in pervious concrete, however. Because pervious mixes are always low in water, compared to most dense-concrete mixes, water reduction is not the goal. Plasticizers are used instead to improve the way the cement paste flows and coats the coarse aggregate.

Viscosity modifiers make the fresh cement paste thicker and stickier. They reduce the risk of draindown. They let you add a little more water without making the paste so thin it drips off the aggregate. When pervious concrete contains a viscosity modifier, you don't have to be quite so precise in getting the water content right.

Retarders slow the chemical reactions that make concrete set. They give you more time to place and compact pervious concrete.

Set stabilizers play the same role as retarders, but with a more extreme effect. While retarders just slow down the chemical reactions with an effect similar to that of cool weather, set stabilizers completely shut down the hardening process for a while. The original purpose of set stabilizers was to save concrete trucks and mixers in emergencies that prevent concrete from being discharged. Pervious concrete has given these admixtures a new purpose. Because unmodified pervious concrete sets fast, ready-mix suppliers rely on set stabilizers to increase the length of time it can be used. Retarders can do the same thing, but set stabilizers provide more time.

Do you need any or all of those admixtures? That's debatable. In the 1970s and 1980s, the Cement and Concrete Association was recommending against admixtures in pervious concrete. Today, in contrast, if you ask a ready-mix supplier for a pervious mix, it is almost sure to contain at least two admixtures. Who's right?

It's just possible they both are. The right answer may depend on how you get your concrete. If you mix concrete on site, as the old recommendations assumed, you can get by without admixtures. If you buy ready-mix concrete, you probably need them.

Except for air entrainers, the admixtures most used in pervious concrete deal with issues related to ready-mix. Plasticizers and viscosity modifiers are often used together to produce a mix workable enough to discharge freely from a ready-mix truck. Retarders and set stabilizers are used so that concrete will still flow after a long haul time and a wait at the job site.

The need for admixtures — except, once again, the air entrainers — goes down in cool weather.

Fibers

Plastic or natural fibers are sometimes added to pervious concrete. Most are made either of polypropylene or cellulose treated to resist chemical attack. Their advocates claim the fibers improve strength and durability. The usual dosage is about 1 lb fibers per cubic yard of concrete (0.6 kg per cubic meter).

Steel fibers, though widely used in dense concrete, don't work in pervious concrete.

Cellulose fibers

Mix proportions

Pervious-concrete mixes fall into two categories: designed mixes and standard recipes. The category generally depends on where the concrete is batched. Ready-mix concrete, batched at a concrete supplier's plant, almost always involves a designed mix. Site-mixed concrete, in contrast, is more often batched to a simple, standard recipe.

Designed mixes

A designed mix is the work of a skilled practitioner who works out the precise proportions of all the components, taking into account not only the project requirements but also the local materials and the capabilities of the concrete supplier. The practitioner usually works for the ready-mix concrete company.

A complete mix design will show the quantities of aggregate and cement in pounds per cubic yard or kilograms per cubic meter. Water quantity usually shows up in gallons or liters, but sometimes it too is in pounds or kilograms. Admixtures, which come in much smaller quantities than the other ingredients, are shown in ounces or milliliters.

The table below shows the usual range of quantities:

Component	Quantity per cubic yard	Quantity per cubic meter
Cement	450-700 lb	270-420 kg
Coarse aggregate	2000-2700 lb	1200-1600 kg
Fine aggregate	0-150 lb	0-90 kg
Water	16-25 gal.	81-144 L

Water-cement ratios in designed mixes typically fall between 0.27 and 0.34.

Standard recipes

These provide a simple way to batch concrete on site. A recipe for dense concrete normally consists of three numerals that show the ratio of cement to fine aggregate to coarse aggregate by mass or volume. A 1:2:4 dense-concrete mix contains one part cement, two parts fine aggregate, and four parts coarse aggregate.

A standard recipe for pervious concrete is even simpler because it contains just two numerals that show the ratio of cement to coarse aggregate. The only common one is 1:4. I've heard of 1:8 mixes, but they weren't used for the wearing surfaces of pavements.

These are the right quantities of coarse aggregate, cement, and water for a 1:4 mix.

Standard recipes almost never show water, though it's essential. That's because the quantity of water poured into the mixer varies according to the aggregate's moisture content and the water left in the mixer from its last washing. It's assumed that the batcher will add as much water as it takes to achieve the desired result — a cement paste wet enough to coat all the rocks, and dry enough not to drip off. The right amount is usually a bit less than half the volume of cement.

Pervious concrete made to a simple ratio recipe generally lacks fine aggregate and admixtures.

Mixing the concrete

The big decision here is whether to order ready-mix or mix the concrete on site. Then there is the important matter of getting the water content right.

Ready-mix concrete

This is batched at a plant and delivered to the job site in trucks. The concrete is normally a designed mix, made to meet a performance specification for void content and other properties. It usually contains admixtures.

Where dense concrete is concerned, ready-mix is the automatic choice for almost every job that requires more than a few cubic feet of material, at least in North America. That choice has carried over into the pervious field.

Any concrete plant that makes dense concrete should be able to handle pervious concrete, too. But certain properties of pervious concrete can cause trouble with ready-mix if you don't allow for them. You need to consider setting time and workability.

Pervious concrete sets fast. If no one pays attention it can set before it leaves the ready-mix truck, and that's not pretty. The normal rules allow 90 minutes (less in hot

A ready-mix plant

Pervious concrete often needs a little help getting down the chute.

weather) to put concrete on the ground after it has been batched, but that can be too long for pervious concrete made without admixtures. If the drive from concrete plant to job site takes more than a few minutes, or if a truck has to wait on site for more than a few minutes before discharging its load, you can get in trouble. Here are some ideas for preventing the problem:

- Choose a ready-mix plant close to the job site.
- Schedule deliveries so trucks can start discharging as soon as they arrive on site.
- Have enough workers and equipment on hand so trucks can be emptied quickly.
- Add a retarder to the mix.
- Add a set stabilizer to the mix.

Workability is an issue because pervious concrete has so little of it. Ready-mix trucks weren't designed for pervious concrete and they have some trouble with its low workability. Compared to a normal dense-concrete mix, pervious concrete leaves the truck more slowly and slides down the chute more reluctantly. Admixtures help, but even with them you should expect a slower pour and some challenges in placing concrete more than a few feet from the back of the ready-mix truck.

Paving contractors who use highly workable dense concrete sometimes pour more than 100 cu yd (80 cu m) per hour. Nobody does that with pervious concrete, though. If you can reach 50 cu yd (40 cu m) per hour, you're doing better than most.

Because pervious concrete is so stiff, it can be hard to place directly from the truck. Here the contractor is using a telescoping belt conveyor to shift the concrete to its final position.

And though ready-mix trucks usually carry several extension chutes for putting the concrete where you want it, you can never use them all with a pervious mix. If you did, the ramp would be too shallow for the concrete to slide down without a lot of help. You might get away with one extension chute, but rarely more. Unless you're making a narrow pour and can get the truck right next to the forms, plan on using wheelbarrows, buggies, or a conveyor.

If concrete arrives too stiff, you can add a little water to increase workability. But you need to take extreme care. The consequences of adding too much water are worse with pervious than with dense concrete. Make sure the truck's drum spins at mixing speed for at least 20 revolutions after each addition of water.

Calculating the amount of concrete to order is the same for pervious and dense concrete. You measure the slab's volume in cubic yards or cubic meters and add 5 to 10%.

Mixing on site

This covers a wide range of practices, from mixing a cubic foot in a wheelbarrow to setting up a mobile batch plant that has almost all the capabilities of a ready-mix location. For the most part, though, we are talking about batches of a few cubic feet made in a portable mixer. Site-mixed concrete is usually made to a standard recipe (though designed mixes are certainly possible), and is not expected to meet a performance specification.

Some books say you should always batch concrete components by mass, not by volume. But in truth I don't know anybody who follows that rule when mixing small batches on site. Everybody batches by volume, and it works. When mixing pervious concrete on site to a standard recipe, follow these steps:

1. Use the same container, or identical containers, for cement and aggregate. Either a bucket or a wood box with handles will work.

2. Size the container so that each batch contains a whole number of containers full of cement or aggregate. If you are making a standard 1:4 mix, then your container needs to be small enough so that five containers worth of material won't overload the mixer. Never use a partly filled container.

3. When measuring out the ingredients, always overfill the container, smack the sides to release air pockets, and strike off excess material with a straight stick.

4. Plan on adding about half as much water as cement, by volume. But don't pour it all in at once. Add water gradually and keep checking the mix till it reaches the consistency and appearance you want.

If you get careless and make the concrete too wet, you can dry it up by adding a little cement and aggregate in the prescribed proportions. That's a luxury you don't normally have with ready-mix.

Few North American contractors mix any concrete on site. No doubt there are good reasons for that. But on pervious jobs site mixing is worth a look, for these reasons:

• It eliminates the ticking clock that comes with every ready-mix truck. Since you don't mix concrete till you're ready to use it, and since you can discharge a mixer quickly, you needn't worry about pervious concrete's fast setting rate.
• It lowers the risk of cold joints, since you place small batches one after the other.
• It reduces the need for admixtures.

One benefit you won't see on that list is lower cost. Mixing your own concrete rarely saves money. When you buy ready-mix you are, roughly speaking, just paying for the materials, and you need those same materials when you mix on site.

Ordering materials for pervious concrete is easier than ordering the ingredients for dense concrete. Figuring aggregate quantities for dense concrete is complicated. You must consider the proportions of coarse and fine aggregates. And then, because of the way the different-size particles pack together, you have order about 52-56% more aggregate, by volume, than the amount of mixed concrete you need. To make 1 cu yd (27 cu ft) of dense concrete, you have to buy about 42 cu ft of aggregates.

But you can forget all that when you mix pervious concrete. The volume of coarse aggregate is almost exactly the same as the volume of the mixed concrete. To get quantities for mixing on site, follow these steps:

1. Figure the volume of the slab (length x width x depth) in cubic yards or cubic meters.

2. Add 10% to allow for compaction and errors. Some people add just 5% if the slab takes over 200 cu yd (150 cu m). The result is the amount of coarse aggregate to order, in cubic yards or cubic meters.

3. Multiply the result of step 2 by the mix ratio. If following a 1:4 ratio, multiply the coarse aggregate volume by 1/4. The result is the amount of cement you need in cubic yards or cubic meters.

4. Multiply the result of step 3 by the number of standard bags found in 1 cu yd or 1 cu m.

5. Round up to the next higher whole number. This is the number of bags of cement to order.

Step 2 gives you a value in cubic yards or cubic meters. When you place your order, it's OK to stick with those units. Even if your supplier sells aggregate by weight, he or she will know how to convert from cubic yards or cubic meters to make sure you get the right volume.

Step 4 requires you to know the size of a standard bag, which varies from country to country. In the US the standard bag weighs 94 lb and holds 1 cu ft. It takes 27 of them to make 1 cu yd. In other countries you may find 50-kg or 25-kg bags. A 50-kg bag holds 33.2 L, and it takes 30 of them to make 1 cu m. A 25-kg bag holds 16.6 L, and it takes 60 of them to make 1 cu m.

Can pervious concrete be mixed by hand? Not finding an answer in the literature and never having seen it done, I tried it in my backyard. I whipped up a 1:4 mix with ordinary Portland cement and 3/4-in. (20-mm) crushed rock. I mixed the dry components first, and then added water.

I am happy to report that it worked. I won't say it was easy; mixing concrete by hand never is. But it wasn't particularly hard. Indeed, I got the distinct impression it was less work than mixing dense concrete. The lighter weight was noticeable. The result, with light compaction, had a 39% void content.

Water content

Whether you order ready-mix or make concrete on site, the water content needs to be just right. If you add too little water, the cement paste won't coat the aggregate properly and some cement may remain dry. If you add too much water, the cement paste will drip off the aggregate.

Regrettably, you can't just measure out a fixed amount of water the way you do with cement and aggregates. There are two reasons for that. One is that the aggregates,

and often the mixer too, already contain some water, but you never know exactly how much. The other is that pervious concrete is highly sensitive to small changes in water content. You can be off a few percent on cement and aggregate and never know it, but water doesn't give you that luxury.

How do you know when you've added just enough water? You rely on your eyes and your hands, and I probably don't have to tell you that experience helps.

Some people judge the water content on appearance alone. They look for a cement paste wet enough to glisten, but not so wet it runs off the aggregate. If the cement looks dry or dull, they add water, carefully, till they see that shine.

Other people prefer to grab a handful of concrete, squeeze it into a ball, and release it. Don't forget to put your gloves on before you try this. If the ball falls apart, the mix is too dry. If the ball slumps, with cement paste flowing out of it, the mix is too wet. If the ball more or less keeps its shape, the mix is just right.

Some people judge water content by forming the concrete into a ball.

When the water content is just right, pervious concrete glistens.

The lab technician is preparing to measure concrete density in the field.

Now that's all very well, but if you've never seen pervious concrete before and are about to make your first batch, you'd probably like a rough idea how much water to put in. Let's do a little figuring.

Good pervious concrete usually has a water-cement ratio between 0.27 and 0.34, by mass. If you are batching by mass, then, as ready-mix plants always do, the right water content will fall between 25 and 32 lb for each standard, 94-lb, bag of cement. In metric units, that would be 27-34 kg water for each 100 kg cement.

If you are batching by volume, assume you'll use between 3.0 and 3.8 US gallons for each standard, 94-lb bag of cement. In metric units, that would be 13.5 to 17.0 L water for each 50-kg bag of cement. If you buy your cement in 25-kg bags, then you'd add 6.8 to 8.5 L water per bag.

When batching by volume in small quantities, you may find it helpful to remember that the volume of water will be roughly half the volume of cement, or a little less. A water-cement ratio of 0.50 by volume translates to 0.33 by mass. Or to look at it the other way, the normal range of 0.27-0.34, for water-cement ratio by mass, works out to 0.41-0.51 when you measure volume instead.

If the mix includes a pozzolan, then the water content should be proportional to the mass or volume of the cement and pozzolan added together. Strictly speaking, this is called not the water-cement ratio, but the water-cementitious ratio or the water-cementitious material ratio.

Concrete testing

Five tests are commonly used to control dense concrete:

    1. the slump test to measure workability;

    2. the crushing of molded cylinders or cubes to measure compressive strength;

    3. measurement of air content to determine amount of entrained air;

    4. temperature;

    5. density (unit weight).

Tests 1-3 are pretty much useless on pervious mixes. Test 4, for temperature, is exactly the same for pervious and impervious concretes. It's straightforward and we needn't spend any time on it. Test 5, for density, is the big one. It's the most useful test for pervious concrete and has its own ASTM test method (ASTM C 1688, 2008).

You can test pervious concrete for slump, but the answer won't tell you anything useful. Most pervious mixes have slumps below 1 in. (25 mm), and the slump test is useless in that low range.

Molded cylinders or cubes are equally useless, but for a different reason. The compressive strength of pervious concrete depends heavily on how well you compact it. While you can compact concrete in a test cylinder, there is no way to know you have matched, or even come close, to the degree of compaction present in the slab. If you need to know pervious concrete's compressive strength, core-drill cylinders after the concrete has hardened.

Density

ASTM C 1688 sets out a detailed test method for measuring the density of fresh pervious concrete. The test is similar to the one used for measuring the density of dense concrete, differing in how the sample is compacted. The test method for dense concrete, ASTM C 138, calls for rodding or vibrating the sample, depending on its slump. Pervious concrete, in contrast, is consolidated by dropping a standard Proctor hammer on it.

The test involves these steps:

    1. Fill a cylindrical mold with fresh concrete, in two equal layers. The mold is the same as that used in a Type B air gauge.

    2. Compact each layer by dropping the Proctor hammer on it 20 times, from a height of 12 in. (305 mm).

    3. Make sure that after compaction the sample sticks up above the rim of the mold.

    4. Strike off the sample flush with the rim.

    5. Weigh the sample.

The test result is the sample's weight (after subtracting the weight of the mold, of course) divided by the volume. It's expressed in pounds per cubic foot or kilogrammes per cubic meter.

When specifications control the density, it's usual to allow a tolerance of plus or minus 5 lb/cu ft (80 kg/cu m). On a recent job in Tennessee, the contract called for 116 lb/cu ft (1860 kg/cu m). The concrete would have been accepted as long as its measured density fell between 111 and 121 lb/cu ft (1780 and 1940 kg/cu m). It did, by the way.

Though the test method as I describe it here remains the law of the land, so to speak, there is some controversy over the use of the Proctor hammer to compact the sample. Stay tuned for changes.

Estimating void content from density

Though the ASTM C 1688 test method does not directly measure void content, it is often used to estimate that essential property. Here is the formula:

$$U = (T-D)/T \times 100\%$$
Where:
U = estimated void content
T = concrete's theoretical density without any air
D = density measured in the field

Void contents estimated from ASTM C 1688 may not match those found in the finished pavement, for two reasons. First, the concrete's theoretical density without air (quantity T in the formula above) may not describe the actual condition of the materials used. Second and more importantly, the degree of compaction provided by the technician's hammer almost certainly differs from that provided by the paving contractor's tools.

Chapter 6
Other Materials

While concrete gets all the publicity, other materials are equally important to the success of a pervious pavement. In this chapter we will look at:

- sub-base materials;
- filter fabrics;
- liners;
- perforated pipe;
- joint filler;
- curing materials;
- accessories.

Sub-base materials

The sub-base performs two functions in a pervious-concrete pavement. First, it supports the concrete slab and distributes loads to the ground. That's the role the sub-base plays in any pavement, dense or pervious. Second, it provides part of the reservoir for stormwater. That role is unique to pervious pavements.

Fortunately the same material, coarse aggregate, serves well for both functions. Any coarse aggregate suitable for making pervious concrete will work for a sub-base, too.

Open-graded coarse aggregate makes a good sub-base for pervious concrete.

But the choice is wider than that. Some aggregates that you wouldn't put in concrete are good enough under the slab. Sub-bases often contain bigger rocks — sometimes even cobbles more than 2 in. (50 mm) across.

Make sure, though, that the sub-base aggregate is coarse, with no more than a trace of fines. Sub-bases under dense concrete often consist of all-in aggregate, also called crusher-run, which contains a blend of coarse and fine particles. That's useless in a pervious pavement, because it has almost no void content.

Close-graded, all-in aggregate is not good under pervious concrete, though it's often used under dense concrete and asphalt.

The sub-base thickness is a design decision. The determining factor may be hydrologic (the need for a stormwater reservoir), or structural (the need to support heavy loads), or related to frost protection.

Not every pervious pavement needs a sub-base. Where the climate is mild or the subgrade highly pervious, sub-bases are often omitted.

Whatever it's made of, the sub-base should be moist when you place concrete over it.

Filter fabrics

Also called geotextiles, these are sheets of flexible plastic full of tiny holes. Their purpose is to let water pass through while keeping fine particles such as silt and clay from migrating into a pavement layer where they don't belong. Some are woven; others consist of solid sheets with holes punched in them. The holes can amount to as much as 30% of the total area, ranging in size from 0.002 to 0.02 in. (0.05 to 0.5 mm).

Filter fabrics vary widely in permeability, from about 10 in./hr (250 mm/hr) up 1000 in./hr (25,000 mm/hr) or more. The materials at the low end of that range are less permeable than pervious concrete. But they are still more pervious than almost any subgrade soil, so they seldom limit the hydrologic design.

Filter fabric normally goes between subgrade and sub-base. If the pavement lacks a sub-base, then the fabric goes between subgrade and slab.

Filter fabric, if used, goes under the sub-base.

Not every pavement needs filter fabric. It's often left out over sandy or rocky subgrades. And it is redundant in any pavement that includes a liner over the subgrade.

Liners

Also called geomembranes, these are flexible sheets that block the flow of water and other liquids. They somewhat resemble filter fabrics and are located similarly within the pavement, but the two products do totally different jobs. Filter fabrics have holes to let water through. Liners have no holes, are impervious, and are used to stop water infiltration.

In most pervious pavements a liner is the last thing you'd want. It's usually better to let water infiltrate the subgrade as freely as possible. In some situations, however, water that passes through the slab should not enter the ground. Examples include:

- brownfield sites with contaminated soil;
- pavements where water is harvested for use;
- livestock-handling facilities.

Liners go on top of the subgrade, and under the slab and sub-base. A liner is normally used along with a drainage system to carry the water off to the side of the pavement.

Perforated pipe

This is used within the sub-base to drain water. You may need it in any of these situations:

- where the ground has a low infiltration rate; over a liner;
- where stormwater is harvested for use.

Perforated pipe

Normally the perforated pipes run in one direction only, parallel to one another. On sloped sites, pipes run at right angles to the slope. Depending on the site, the perforated pipes may run to collectors made of plain, unperforated pipe.

Sometimes trenches dug into the subgrade and filled with aggregate can replace perforated pipes for drainage.

Joint filler

This is a sheet of compressible material used to form isolation and expansion joints. Joint filler is meant to separate a concrete slab from another slab, from another pavement type, or from something else like a building foundation or wall. It lets the separated items move slightly without putting undue stress on each other. Joint filler is also known as filler board or, less accurately, expansion strip.

Joint fillers are made of several materials that look different but don't vary that much in performance. The most common filler consists of plant fibers imbedded in resin.

Curing materials

Curing is the process of keeping new concrete moist so the hardening process can continue. The standard curing material for pervious slabs is polyethylene sheet, applied soon after concrete placement and left on for seven days. It comes in clear, white, and black. White's a good choice in hot, sunny weather. Any color will do in cool weather.

Polyethylene sheet is the standard curing material.

Here black and white curing sheets have been used on the same job, for no good reason. Normally you'd use black in cold weather, and white in hot.

Polyethylene sheet sometimes leaves dark and light streaks on the slab surface. If that's unacceptable, you can use a two-layer curing sheet that consists of an absorbent fabric bonded to polyethylene. The absorbent layer goes on the bottom.

Curing compounds — liquids that form a film over the concrete — have no place on pervious concrete. If applied thick enough to provide an effective cure, they would seal the surface and leave it impervious.

Though regular curing compounds are of no use, some contractors spray on a vegetable oil right after concrete placement to reduce early drying. The oil doesn't replace polyethylene, but is used in addition to it. The same oil comes in handy for coating tools and forms so concrete doesn't stick to them.

Accessories

Many pavements include accessories that attach to or in some way work with the concrete slab.

Curbs
Curbs are slightly controversial in the field of pervious concrete. Some authorities recommend against them (Ferguson 2005, 42; Sparkman 2009), on the grounds that a functioning pervious pavement doesn't need them. The main purpose of a curb is to channel runoff, and pervious concrete eliminates runoff under normal conditions.

Still many pervious pavements get curbs. Custom explains some of them, but there are practical reasons, too. Curbs keep vehicles off sidewalks and lawns. Used around landscape plantings, curbs can reduce the amount of topsoil and mulch that washes out over the pavement. In some cases contractors use curbs, or the gutters attached to them, as side forms when placing the pervious concrete.

The standard curb-and-gutter is rarely essential around pervious concrete, but some people use it anyway. This is a parking lot in Morristown, Tennessee.

Here a curb (minus the gutter) serves as the side form for a pervious-concrete pour. This detail only works when a laser screed is used to strike off.

Wheelstops

These are raised strips that stop drivers from going off the edge of a pavement when parking their cars. Sometimes they are also used in the middle of a lot where cars park nose to nose. They keep vehicles off lawns and flowerbeds, and they may stop cars from getting stuck in soft ground or steep slopes. But since drivers can get over them with a bit of effort, they cannot replace guardrails where real danger is involved.

Wheelstops made of precast concrete.

Wheelstops are available in precast concrete or recycled plastic. Heavy timbers have also been used.

Some manufacturers offer a choice of hardware for attaching the wheelstops to either dense concrete or asphalt. They don't sell anchors specifically for pervious concrete, but the concrete anchors seem to work.

Wheelstops made of recycled plastic.

Paint

Parking lots and roadways often need striping and other markings to define parking spaces and direct traffic. Ordinary marking paint will work, though it generally looks fainter on pervious concrete than on dense concrete or asphalt. Tape does not work well.

If applied too thickly, paint can seal the surface and make it impervious. Such sealing is unlikely to cause much trouble if confined to widely spaced stripes. But beware the risk when covering large areas. The photo below shows a handicapped-parking stall that is heavily sealed with paint.

When striping for parking stalls, it's important to get the dimensions right. In the United States the standard stall is 9 ft (2.7 m) wide and 18 or 20 ft (5.5 or 6.1 m) long. Stalls reserved for compact cars are the same width but only 15 ft (4.6 m) long. A good size for a motorcycle stall is 4.5 x 8 ft (1.4 x 2.4 m) (Cottrell 2008, 3-4).

Bollards and railings

On dense concrete, people sometimes mount bollards and railings directly on the slab, using anchor bolts. That's unwise on pervious concrete, which tends to have lower and more variable strength than its dense counterpart. The bolts might come loose.

The safe way to mount bollards and railings is to run them straight through the concrete slab and imbed them in a footing made of dense concrete. You have three options for getting the accessory through the slab. You can install

You can paint markings on pervious concrete, but the results aren't always as crisp as with dense concrete or asphalt.

the accessory first and cast pervious concrete around it. You can leave a hole in the pervious concrete, forming it up with a paperboard tube or something similar. Or you can core-drill through the concrete after is has set.

Bike racks

These take a wide range of forms. But when considering how to mount them, they fall into two types.

Some bike racks rest on a wide bottom and don't necessarily have to be fixed to the pavement. If they are fixed, it's to keep them from shifting in use or from being stolen. This type can be bolted to a pervious-concrete pavement without much risk of damage.

The others rest on a small base and must be bolted down firmly to stop them tipping over. This type should not be mounted directly on pervious concrete. One solution is to pour a pad of dense concrete and bolt the bike rack to it. Another option is to support the rack on a separate footing below the pervious slab — but be warned that some standard racks aren't tall enough for that.

With any rack, you need a space about 2 x 6 ft (0.6 x 1.8 m) for each bike.

Lighting

Lighting engineers often take into account the pavement's reflectance when deciding how much illumination to provide. Precise measurements aren't needed, and aren't even particularly useful since reflectance changes as pavements age.

Some designers rely on a system in which surfaces are divided into four categories according to their lighting requirements (Stark 1986, 42).

Pavement classification for lighting (Roadway 1983, 7)

Class	Typical materials	Reflectance mode
R1	Dense concrete	Mostly diffuse
R2	Asphalt with brightener	Diffuse and specular
R3	Ordinary asphalt	Slightly specular
R4	Very smooth asphalt	Mostly specular

What class does pervious concrete belong in? The standard lighting guides don't say, but I'd argue that R3 fits best. If the concrete has been deliberately brightened with slab or white cement (perhaps to meet an SRI value for LEED points), then R2 is probably appropriate.

Chapter 7
Construction

Building a pervious concrete pavement typically involves these steps:

1. Prepare the subgrade.
2. Lay the sub-base, along with any auxiliary sub-slab materials.
3. Set forms.
4. Transport and place the concrete.
5. Strike off and compact the concrete.
6. Joint the slab.
7. Cure the concrete.

In this chapter we will look at all those steps, in just that order.

Subgrade preparation

The key here is to do as little as possible to the natural ground. You have to remove topsoil and tree roots, and every site requires at least a little grading. But when doing all that you should try hard not to compact the subgrade. Overcompaction — any compaction, for that matter — reduces the site's infiltration rate.

This goes against normal construction practice, in which compaction is considered a good thing. You cannot overcompact the subgrade when preparing for dense concrete or dense asphalt — the more, the better. But subgrade compaction is the enemy when building a pervious pavement.

Preventing overcompaction
This is easier said than done. One way is to avoid motorized equipment, but that's hardly practical on anything bigger than a sidewalk. When using heavy equipment, you may be tempted to spread the traffic out over the site to reduce its effect. Avoid that temptation. It's better to stick to a defined route, even if you have to repair it later. That way the overcompaction will be limited in area, and you will know where it is.

Complicating the problem, much overcompaction takes place before the pavement contractor even shows up on the job. Housing subdivisions are often prepared by a process called mass grading in which the whole area is graded and compacted in one go. To prevent overcompaction on such sites is impractical (Lichter 1994, 129). On some projects the only answer is to fence off the areas that get pervious concrete so other trades can't operate there.

If you find yourself facing an overcompacted subgrade, whether from construction traffic or from earlier usage, can you loosen it? The answer seems to be yes, but more research is needed. Though equipment exists to rip or cultivate even badly compacted soil, it was designed not for paving but to help plants grow (Bradshaw 1995, 72-73, and Rolf 1994, 131-148). The loosened soil may lack the stability a pavement needs.

Grading
Part of the subgrade preparation is grading — making it level or setting it to the right slope, as the design requires. Avoid deep fills and deep cuts wherever you can, because they both cause problems. With deep fills the problem is compaction. Some compaction is needed to avoid severe settlement later. But it's easy to go too far and reduce permeability. With deep cuts the risk is that you will remove the relatively loose upper layers and expose dense, impervious material.

Perhaps the trickiest grading occurs on sloped sites where the design calls for terracing to increase reservoir capacity. Terraces are among those details that look better on the engineer's drawings than in the field.

Laying the sub-base

Not every pavement gets a sub-base. Designers often omit sub-bases in mild climates where the subgrade is permeable.

If the design calls for a liner or filter fabric, this it the time to install it. Liners and filters normally go between the subgrade and sub-base.

Placing the sub-base is usually a simple task, but you need to watch out for a couple of things. First, try not to overcompact the subgrade with the equipment used to transport and spread the sub-base aggregate. (Is this starting to sound familiar?). Second, be sure to maintain the design thickness. Making the sub-base too thick does no harm, but making it too thin reduces the reservoir capacity, and can compromise both the hydrologic and structural designs.

Unlike the close-graded aggregates often used under dense pavements, the open-graded stone that serves as the normal sub-base for pervious concrete needs no compaction.

The last step in preparing the sub-base is to wet it thoroughly just before you place concrete. If there's no sub-base, wet the subgrade instead. Never place pervious concrete over a dry base that will suck water from it.

This sub-base is almost ready to be covered with pervious concrete.

Formwork

Forms have two roles. They define the slab's edges, and with some construction methods they have to support the tools used to strike off and compact the concrete.

Steel and wood forms both do a good job. But if you plan to use the traditional strip-and-roll method that relies on battens nailed to the tops of the forms, wood is your only option.

Steel forms

Wood forms

If the pavement abuts a curb-and-gutter combination, you can use the gutter as the side form. But most pervious pavements don't need curbs and gutters.

Some pavement designs call for a vertical curb with no attached gutter. In that case you can use the curb as a form, but only if you are striking off with a laser screed. Other strike-off tools require a form that's set to the finished pavement grade, and a plain curb doesn't provide that.

You can, in certain situations, place pervious concrete without forms. You just put the concrete on the ground and roll it out, leaving the edges rough. The resulting rustic look can be just right for a country driveway or footpath.

Transporting and placing

Concrete either arrives in a ready-mix truck or comes out of a mixer somewhere on site. Either way, you have to transport it those last few feet — and sometimes more than a few feet — to its final location in the slab. Most methods for transporting dense concrete work with pervious, including:

- placing straight from the ready-mix truck, also called tailgating;
- power buggies;
- wheelbarrows;
- belt conveyors.

Concrete pumps do not make the list, however. Pervious concrete is too stiff to go through any normal pump. Builders placing pervious concrete tend to use telescoping belt conveyors in situations where dense concrete would be pumped. Unlike pumps, conveyors handle stiff mixes with ease.

Placing concrete straight from the ready-mix truck is practical on narrow pours where you can pull the truck right up to the forms.

Pouring straight from the ready-mix truck is an attractive option, but it's a little harder with pervious concrete. Pervious mixes come out of the truck slowly, and the discharge chute needs to be steep. With high-slump dense concrete you can attach multiple extension chutes to the truck, allowing discharge several yards away.

Forget about that with pervious concrete. You'll be lucky if you can use even one extension chute, in addition to the chute that's always attached to the truck. Even then you may find yourself helping the concrete down with shovel or come-along.

A telescoping belt conveyor

The belt conveyor reaches out over the pour and drops the concrete through a heavy rubber hose.

No matter how the concrete is transported, the final placement still calls for hand tools — typically square-end shovels, rakes, or come-alongs. This is where concrete workers earn their pay. Placing concrete is always hard work, and placing pervious concrete is especially hard.

Every placing method still requires some hand labor.

Strike-off and compaction

Once the concrete is on the ground, you need to strike it off and compact it. Striking-off sets the concrete to grade and scrapes off the excess. Compaction, also called consolidation, reduces some of the concrete's air voids to increase its density and strength.

Depending on the method, these can be separate steps or combined into one operation. The choices are:

- strip-and-roll;
- powered roller screed;
- laser screed with roller head;
- slip-form road paver.

Strip-and-roll

This is the traditional method, and it's still a good one. It involves these steps:

1. Nail battens (thin wood strips) to the forms.
2. Strike off the concrete flush with the tops of the battens, using either a hand straightedge or a vibrating screed.
3. Remove the battens.
4. Push a heavy roller across the slab till the concrete has been pressed down flush with the forms. The roller must be long enough to reach from form to form.
5. Push a short cross-roller over the floor at right angles to the roller used in step 4.

Some people hand-tamp the slab edges between steps 3 and 4.

Plywood shims have been mounted under both ends of the vibrating screed.

Striking off with a shimmed-up vibrating screed

Hand rolling

In pace of the battens nailed to the forms, you can attach shims under both ends of the strike-off toll used in step 2. Shims work better with a vibrating screed than with a hand straightedge.

Some contractors tamp the edges by hand.

What's the right thickness for the battens or shims? It's often about 1/2 in. (12 mm), but the answer varies from job to job, and you may need a bit of trial and error to find out. Too thin, and the concrete will be weak. Too thick, and the roller won't press the concrete down to the level of the forms, resulting in a dip at the slab edge.

Some contractors wouldn't dream of doing a strip-and-roll job without using a vibrating screed in step 2, but that tool is less essential than you might guess. On dense concrete, vibrating screeds are valued for their compacting ability. On pervious concrete, in contrast, rollers do most of the compacting, and the vibrating screed's role is mainly one of convenience, to make the strike-off easier. You can do a good job with a hand straightedge, but it takes more muscle.

Cross-rolling

The roller for step 4 needs to be both heavy and straight. Opinions vary on the ideal weight, but 30 lb/ft (45 kg/m) is a good starting point. If you can't compact the concrete flush with the forms in at most six passes, either the roller is too light or the battens are too thick. A bent roller will compact the concrete in a washboard pattern with alternating bands of over- and undercompacted material. Some say the deviation from straight should not exceed 1/16 in. (1.5 mm), but I'm not sure that's a realistic goal.

Powered roller screed

This method relies on the roller screed, a motorized steel tube that spins at high speed. You pull the roller screed slowly over the slab, with its end riding on the side forms. As you pull it in one direction, the motor is trying to pull it the other way. The spinning tube then strikes the concrete off level with the forms, flicking the excess ahead as it goes.

Some rollers can run in reverse. That's useful if you find low spots after the first pass, because you can back over them to fill them up.

Running a cross-roller at right angles to the roller screed improves flatness and adds a little compaction.

Keep rollers wet with oil (shown here) or water so concrete doesn't stick to them.

Laser screed with roller head

The heart of this method is the Somero Laser Screed, fitted with a special head designed for pervious concrete. Unlike the vibrating or roller screed riding on the forms, a laser screed strikes off to a grade determined by a laser level. Since it operates independently of the forms, it works on slabs of almost any width.

The laser screed strikes off independently of the forms.

The business end of the screed consists of an auger and two rollers. The auger does the main work of striking-off. The first roller spins under power, just like a roller screed. It can be set slightly lower than the auger. The second roller is unpowered and articulated so it rests on the concrete under its own weight.

The business end of a laser screed consists of an auger, a powered rolled, and an unpowered roller.

The cross-roller is used after the laser screed, as in other methods. But here its main purpose is to smooth the seams between laser-screed passes.

A cross-roller smoothes out the seams between passes of the laser screed.

Slip-form paver

This method holds much promise for big parking lots and roads, but for now we have to regard it as still under development. A slip-form paver is a big machine that crawls on tracks, laying a wide strip of concrete as it goes. Steel plates attached to the paver slide over the concrete, forming the slab's top and sides.

The strip in the center was placed with a slip-form paver. The strips on either side were placed by the strip-and-roll method.

Though slip-form pavers routinely handle stiff, dense-concrete mixes, they need modifications to work well on pervious concrete. The one in the photograph was fitted with extra weights to stop it from riding up.

A slip-form paver

Jointing

Many pavements contain joints for crack control. But some don't, either because they are so small that cracks are unlikely, or because the designers decided that cracks would be acceptable. Crack-control joints fall into four categories according to the way they are made:

- formed joints, also known as construction joints;
- insert joints;
- sawn joints;
- rolled joints.

Formed joints are made by stopping the pour at a side form. The slab on the other side of the joint is poured another day.

Insert joints are made by pouring the concrete around strips of wood or other solid material. Inserts cost more and involve more work than sawn or rolled joints, but they provide a decorative touch that some pavements need.

Sawn joints are made by cutting the slab with a concrete saw after it has set. The sawcut normally goes one fourth of the way through the slab, though some people recommend more or less depth than that. Both downcutting and upcutting (Soff-Cut brand) saws have been used successfully on pervious concrete.

A sawn joint

Rolled joints are made with a special joint roller, sometimes called a pizza cutter. It looks just like a cross roller, except it has a fin in the center to press a groove into the concrete.

A joint roller, also called a pizza cutter

Curing

This is the process of keeping concrete moist so the hardening process can continue. Without curing, concrete will set but will never reach its full potential strength. Good curing practices are especially important with pervious concrete because it dries out fast.

The standard curing method consists of covering the slab with a flexible sheet of impervious material. The sheet is usually polyethylene, but some people prefer a composite sheet consisting of absorbent fabric bonded to polyethylene. Seams should be well lapped or taped, with everything weighted down so it can't blow off. Curing compounds aren't safe on pervious concrete because they could seal the surface.

Timing matters. Curing should begin as soon as the concrete has been compacted. Some specifications call for no more than 20 minutes between placement and the start of curing. Truth be told, you can stretch that in cool or damp weather — but it's still a good target. On big slabs you can't wait till the end of the pour to begin curing; you have to do it in stages.

Curing sheets typically stay on at least 7 days. Don't leave them that long without inspection, though. A storm could dislodge them, or other trades could damage them. There's no harm, and a little benefit, in going longer than 7 days if you can.

Some contractors apply vegetable oil to the concrete before covering it up. Oil's advocates say it enhances the cure and prevents the light and dark streaks that polyethylene can leave on concrete. Unlike membrane-forming curing compounds, oil does not seal the surface.

Curing starts right after cross-rolling.

Chapter 8
Problems

In this chapter we will look at some of the problems that afflict pervious concrete, both during construction and later. Problems include:

- draindown;
- raveling;
- cold joints;
- cracking;
- sealing;
- clogging.

Draindown

This occurs during construction when cement paste drips off the aggregate. It's caused by too much water. Usually that's the result of a mistake in batching, but rain on the fresh concrete has a similar effect. Draindown has two bad consequences.

The more obvious is that the slab surface becomes starved of cement. That leaves it weak, and vulnerable to raveling under traffic.

The more insidious consequence is that cement paste collects in the slab's lower levels, filling the holes there. That results in a sealed slab with a much-reduced ability to infiltrate water.

To prevent draindrown, don't add too much water to the mix, and consider the use of a viscosity modifier. Oh, and try not to pour in the rain, but you already knew that.

Raveling

Pervious concrete ravels when aggregate particles break free from it. The usual cause is traffic acting on a surface that lacks the strength to support it. It is particularly likely where motor vehicles turn sharply — in the drive lanes of a parking lot, for example — and where snowplows scrape. Draindown increases the risk of raveling because it leaves the surface starved of cement.

Severe raveling near a joint.

It seems plausible that frost damage could cause raveling, because it does so in dense concrete. However, no one has yet pointed out an example of a pervious-concrete pavement damaged in this way.

Poor compaction at the slab surface makes raveling more likely. Sometimes a whole pavement suffers from this defect. At other times it's confined to slab edges.

Raveling often appears at sawcut joints, rolled joints, cold joints, and cracks, even when the rest of the slab looks good. It's not clear which method of jointing — sawing or rolling — causes more trouble. Bad raveling has occurred with both. But cracks ravel less than joints, pretty consistently.

Many pervious-concrete pavements — most, I'd say — experience a little raveling in their first few weeks. It seems there are always a few stones that are not firmly attached to the rest. That's nothing to be alarmed at, provided the extent of the raveling remains small.

The prevention of raveling takes two paths: making the surface strong, and reducing abrasive traffic. Here are some ways to strengthen the surface:

• Compact the concrete on top as much as you can without sealing it. Alan Sparkman of the Tennessee Concrete Association suggests that a few small sealed areas should be acceptable because they show the surface is as strong as possible (Sparkman 2009). Take special care at slab edges.

• Avoid draindown. Consider using a viscosity modifier for this purpose.

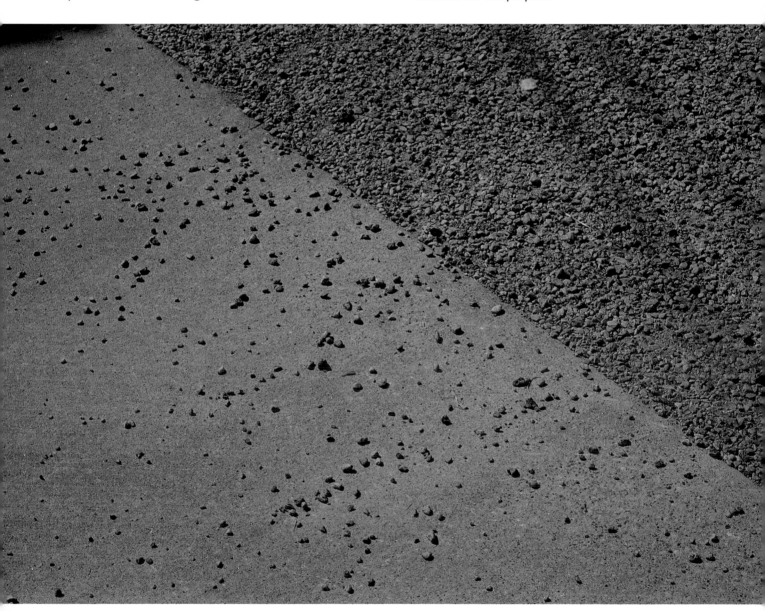

This pavement has raveled all over, with loose aggregate spilling onto the adjacent dense concrete.
This is pervious asphalt, but the same sort of failure can occur on pervious concrete

• Start curing as soon as possible and make sure the concrete stays moist throughout the curing period.

Protecting the pavement from abrasive traffic is harder, since to a large extent the traffic is what it is. Still, we have a few options:

• Protect the new pavement from construction traffic, which is often worse than anything the concrete will have to withstand in later use.
• Switch to dense concrete or asphalt in areas that will experience high wear. Some parking lots have drive lanes made of impervious materials, reserving pervious concrete for the parking stalls.
• Tell snowplow drivers to raise their blades.

It's likely that grinding reduces raveling, because a ground-down surface doesn't have any aggregate particles sticking up.

Can raveling be repaired? Mostly it isn't repaired. It's just accepted as normal wear and tear. You can patch badly raveled areas with more pervious concrete, but it needs to be cured and protected from traffic for several days. Other patching materials should be used with great caution, since most will seal the surface.

Cold joints

These are discontinuities caused by a delay in the concrete pour or, less often, by a change in the concrete mix from batch to batch. They look bad, and they sometimes ravel because one side lacks proper compaction. Some cold joints crack, but in many of those cases it's likely the cold joint merely attracted a crack that would have occurred nearby anyway.

A cold joint

To prevent cold joints, match the concrete placing rate to the concrete delivery rate. If you can put down three truckloads an hour, then you should schedule trucks to arrive 20 minutes apart — no more, no less. Take particular care to avoid waiting a long time for that last batch of the day. It's tempting to wait till you have almost poured out before calculating and ordering the final truckload, but that's a good way to get a cold joint.

Admixtures that delay setting — retarders and set stabilizers — help in preventing cold joints, but cannot substitute for good timing. Cool weather also helps. Despite their name, cold joints are more likely in hot weather.

Cracking

It will surprise no one when I say that concrete cracks. Dense concrete cracks, and so does pervious concrete. Most of the sorts of cracking that afflict dense-concrete slabs also occur in pervious concrete (crazing is an exception), but not in the same proportions. The types most likely to affect pervious concrete are plastic-shrinkage cracks, drying-shrinkage cracks, and structural cracks.

Plastic-shrinkage cracks

These occur while the concrete is still plastic; that is, before it has set. Caused by rapid drying of the slab surface, they are most likely to occur when the evaporation rate is high. Hot weather, sunshine, and — worst of all — high wind all increase the risk.

Pervious concrete is highly vulnerable to plastic-shrinkage cracks, due to its low water content, open texture, and lack of bleed water. (Bleed water is free water in the concrete mix that migrates upward, sometimes appearing at the slab surface as a damp sheen or even a puddle. It's common with dense concrete, and rare with pervious.)

Any of the following steps will help prevent plastic-shrinkage cracks:

- Moisten the sub-base or subgrade (if exposed) before placing concrete.
- Shield the fresh concrete from wind.
- Place concrete in the cool of the night or early morning.
- Spray an evaporation retardant on the fresh concrete. Some contractors use a soybean-oil product for this purpose.
- Spray a fine water mist upwind of the fresh concrete. The mist must be light — almost a fog. Don't use an ordinary hose nozzle, because it will wash cement paste off the aggregate. Use a special misting head.
- Start curing as soon as possible.

Drying-shrinkage cracks

Plastic-shrinkage cracks occur on the day of the pour or not at all. Drying-shrinkage cracks, in contrast, appear later, sometimes weeks later, after the concrete has set and has begun to dry out.

Their main cause, as the name suggests, is drying shrinkage. Concrete starts out wet and gradually dries. As it dries, it gets smaller — or tries to. A slab suspended in midair would just shrink and no harm would come to it. But a slab sitting on the ground is restrained by friction, and sometimes by other factors, such as imbedded hardware. The combination of shrinkage and restraint tries to pull the slab apart, and often succeeds. The result is a drying-shrinkage crack.

Because concrete shrinks as it cools, temperature changes add to the shrinkage stresses that cause cracks. Cracks caused by thermal contraction look just like drying-shrinkage cracks.

Compared to dense-concrete slabs, pervious slabs develop fewer drying-shrinkage cracks. One reason for that difference is that pervious concrete only shrinks about half as much as it dries. Another possible reason is that pervious concrete doesn't curl much.

Slabs of dense concrete undergo a shrinkage-related change called curling or warping. As they dry from the top down, they curl up at the edges. Curling greatly increases the likelihood of cracks and causes other problems.

Curling does not appear to affect pervious concrete much, however. Though I can't find any published study on the matter, my own observations suggest that pervious-concrete slabs curl little, if at all.

There is only one way to prevent drying-shrinkage cracks in pervious concrete, though it's not guaranteed. Install joints to break the slab up into a collection of smaller panels. If each panel is small enough, the shrinkage stresses within it will remain below the critical value and the concrete will not crack.

But stop and think before you get out the pizza cutter or the concrete saw to make all those joints. Are you sure you want joints crisscrossing your pervious slab? A joint and a crack are both breaks in the concrete, with similar effects on the pavement's durability. Joints cost more and seem to ravel more under traffic. In the end it comes down to what looks better, and that's a matter of taste. I vote for cracks. To my eye a few drying-shrinkage cracks in a pervious-concrete pavement don't look bad at all. But many people disagree.

If you do choose joints, please understand that they don't always work. No matter how carefully you make the joints and how closely you space them, sometimes concrete just cracks where it wants.

Drying-shrinkage crack in a slab without crack-control joints

Structural cracks

These occur from overloading, subgrade settlement, or subgrade heaving. The causes, and the methods to prevent them, are the same as for dense concrete.

The keys to preventing structural cracks are good structural design, attention to subgrade and sub-base, and adherence to the specified slab thickness. And there's one thing more: making sure not to overload the slab with construction equipment. That's a real risk for light-duty pavement like footpaths, which may not be designed for any vehicle loads at all.

Sealing

This is the creation of an impervious layer on or within the concrete slab. Sealing usually occurs at the slab surface. Overcompaction or the improper use of trowels and floats seals the top of the slab with cement paste. Paint and curing compounds can also seal pervious concrete. Draindown causes sealing too, but here the problem occurs at the bottom of the slab.

The surface here is sealed with cement paste.

The painter got carried away, sealing the surface.

The following steps will help reduce sealing:

- Don't overcompact the surface.
- Don't finish the surface with floats or trowels.
- Use paint sparingly.
- Don't use curing compound. Cure under sheet materials instead.
- Avoid pavement sealers.

Though sealing is not a good thing, we need to tolerate a bit of it. The gap between over- and undercompaction is narrow. If you compact a slab so lightly that no sealing occurs anywhere, you run the risk of not compacting it enough and leaving it vulnerable to raveling and other problems. Sealing that covers just a few square inches here and there will not ruin a pavement, and ought not to be grounds for rejection.

If the amount of sealing gets out of hand, you can sometimes correct it by grinding. Grinding dramatically changes the concrete's appearance, however.

Clogging

This occurs when debris fills the pores within pervious concrete. The debris can be organic or inorganic. Organic debris comes mainly from tree leaves and grass clippings. Inorganic debris consists mainly of sand, silt, and clay washed onto the pavement from open ground nearby.

The surface here is clogged with plant debris.

These steps can reduce clogging:

- Don't let trees and shrubs hang over pervious concrete.
- Clean up fallen leaves and grass clippings before they decompose.

- Don't let runoff from open ground flow onto pervious concrete. Use a swale or ditch on the pavement's high side if necessary.
- Don't use sand or ashes for winter traction.
- Don't store mulch on pervious concrete.

You can store mulch on top of pervious concrete if you want to, but don't complain when the surface becomes clogged.

As with sealing, it helps to turn a blind eye to a certain amount of clogging. I would never chop down a tree, or forego planting one, just to keep leaves off a pervious pavement. (I would avoid storing mulch on it, though.) Even after severe clogging, pervious concrete takes in more water than does dense concrete or asphalt. Two of the pavements featured as examples in Chapter 9 — the sidewalk in Knoxville and the sloped footpath at Morris Dam State Park — still perform well despite heavy clogging.

And clogging can be reversed, at least to some extent. Vacuuming removes much clogging debris. It works best if you do it often, before the materials work their way far beneath the surface. Pressure washing is even more effective, and has restored some badly clogged pavements to like-new condition.

Interestingly, the risk of clogging seems to be low on high-speed road pavements because suction from truck tires keeps the pores clean.

This surface is clogged with soil from the adjacent open ground.

Chapter 9
Examples

In this last chapter we will look at a few examples of pervious concrete in the real world. My goal here is descriptive, not prescriptive. I'm not trying to tell you what do to (not in this chapter, anyway). I'm just showing you what some people actually did.

A sidewalk

This sidewalk runs in front of Fountain City Elementary School in Knoxville, Tennessee. It dates from 2003, making it about six years old when I photographed it.

A six-year-old sidewalk in Knoxville, Tennessee

The sidewalk surface looks good after six years, with no sign of raveling.

Construction methods were basic. Concrete was placed from a wheelbarrow and compacted with a garden roller (Sparkman 2009). Slab thickness is 4 in. (100 mm), as usual for American sidewalks. There are no crack-control joints.

This pavement has suffered a bit of structural damage. Some edges have broken off, but the damage is minor and has not restricted usage.

A few small edge breaks have occurred.

Much of the sidewalk looks heavily clogged. Some spots even have grass growing on them. Despite that, a school employee told me the pavement never ponds, even in heavy rainstorms.

Some areas are clogged.

A footpath in a hard-wet-freeze zone

Though wide enough to serve as a shared-use path, this pavement at the Morton Arboretum in northern Illinois is clearly meant for foot traffic. It was less than a year old, and part of it was still under construction, when I photographed it in 2009.

It consists of 4 in. (100 mm) of pervious concrete over a coarse stone sub-base, over filter fabric. The sub-base is not nearly as deep as that sometimes recommended for frost protection. It will be interesting to see how this pavement, located in a hard-wet-freeze zone, fares in years to come.

Mottling from the polyethylene sheet cure is very obvious here.

The footpath at the Morton Arboretum is unusually bright and shows a mottled pattern from the polyethylene-sheet cure.

Showing the way

This footpath doesn't really go anywhere, but it points the way to the future. Located on the Indiana State Fairgrounds in Indianapolis, its whole purpose is to educate the public about pervious paving. It includes a small fountain that spills water onto two concrete pads — one dense, the other pervious — to show how differently the two materials handle water. Unfortunately, the fountain was shut down when I visited. I presume it operates when the fair is under way. Signs explain what pervious concrete is and how it helps improve water quality.

Though the overall exhibit, called Pathway to Water Quality, is older, the pervious-concrete path dates from 2005, making it four years old when I photographed it.

Projects like this introduce pervious concrete to people who would never read about it in a newspaper or magazine. Even where pavements weren't built purely for education, signs that explain what pervious concrete does can be useful. Without such signs, many people will pay no attention to what they are walking or driving on and won't notice it isn't ordinary concrete or asphalt.

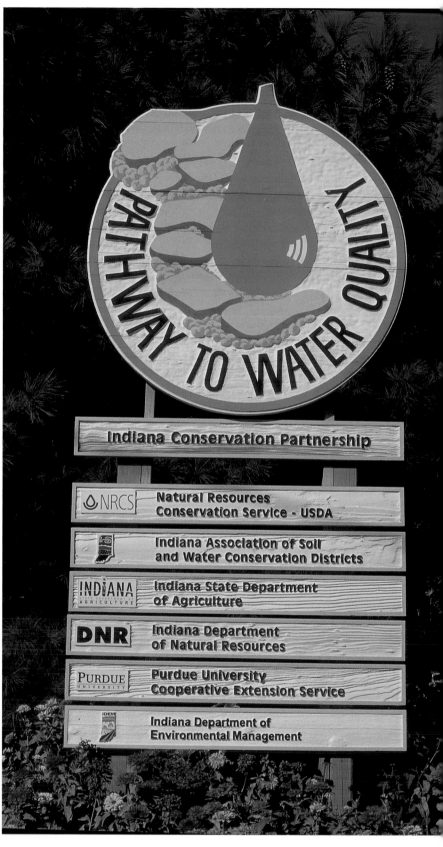

Signs at the Indiana State Fairgrounds explain the role of pervious concrete in controlling water pollution.

The pervious-concrete footpath at the Indiana State Fairgrounds

A masonry border adds to the visual appeal.

A shared-use path half a mile long

Located in a country park near Athens, Tennessee, this path encircles a pond and runs alongside a creek. I understand pavement was allowed here only on the condition that it not increase runoff into the pond and creek.

Athens has a wet-freeze environment with about 90 freeze-thaw cycles a year. The main pavement dates from 2003, making it about 6 years old when I photographed it. An extension to the path is newer.

The pavement consists of 5 in. (125 mm) of pervious concrete over another 5 in. (125 mm) of aggregate sub-base. The subgrade is clay.

Concrete was laid by the strip-and-roll method. When forming the curved sections, the contractor did not bend the forms but instead used multiple short, straight pieces. The result is perhaps less elegant than a pure curve, but it works in this environment. Transverse joints are spaced roughly

Pedestrians were the only users during my visit, though the path is well suited for cyclists, too, with its 10-ft (3.0-m) width. Motor vehicles are forbidden, though not blocked by any physical barrier. The path is equipped with several trashcans, and I bet the workers who empty them drive some kind of truck.

The path has held up well, but its lower reaches were heavily clogged in the fall of 2009. Moss was growing in some spots. I may have seen it at its worst, however. Heavy rains had come through just a couple of weeks before, causing the creek to flood much of the path several feet deep. I could still see the high-water mark on trees and shrubs. Little or no clogging was visible in those parts of the pavement that had stayed above the floodwaters.

A sign in Athens, Tennessee, tells visitors what they are walking or cycling on.

Curved sections were formed up with straight boards. This makes it easier to use the strip-and-roll method.

Low areas of the Athens shared-use path were badly clogged in the fall of 2009.

Breaking the rules

Some experts say you shouldn't place pervious concrete on a steep slope. And some say you shouldn't locate pervious concrete where falling leaves can cause clogging.

The designers of this short shared-use path didn't listen to that advice, and they got away with it.

This is part of a walking route behind a museum at the Norris Dam State Park, in northeastern Tennessee. The route goes down a steep slope that was subject to erosion and was hard for some walkers to navigate safely. Pervious concrete solved both problems, while protecting the small, clean stream that lies at the bottom of the slope.

The footpath at Norris Dam State Park is unusually steep and goes through a heavily wooded area.

The path goes through a densely wooded area, with deciduous trees hanging over the pavement. The result is a heavily clogged surface that supports a healthy crop of moss. That sounds bad, but the concrete still absorbs water. When I observed it during and after a short, heavy shower, I saw no water running off. I found the traction good, though it looked slippery with that wet moss on it.

Located in a wet-freeze climate, the pavement dates from 2004, making it five years old when I photographed it.

Leaves cover the pavement at Norris Dam State Park.

Below:
The lower part of the Norris Dam path is clogged and supports a healthy crop of moss. Despite that, it was safe to walk on minutes after a rainstorm.

Parking for a small professional office

I love this pavement for its modesty. It's not a showy public project. It wasn't built by a government agency or big institution. It's just a few parking spaces in front and back of a small dental office. It lacks curbs and drains. Indeed, its only accessories are paint stripes and wheelstops.

The use of pervious concrete let the owner avoid stormwater fees. The pavement looks like new, except for one small corner break where it fans out to meet the dense-concrete driveway.

The project is located near Nashville, Tennessee, in a wet-freeze climate.

The About Face clinic in Mount Juliet, Tennessee, has a parking lot made of pervious concrete. Note how dark the pervious concrete looks compared to the dense-concrete driveway in the foreground. The difference in brightness is not always this great.

Parking stall at the About Face clinic.

A parking lot that combines pervious and dense concrete

Two parking lots built in 2009 are part of the Cincinnati Zoo's plan to end its reliance on the city sewer system (McD 2009, 1). The total area amounts to slightly less than one acre, but it's not all pervious concrete. The drive aisles, each 20 ft (6.1 m) wide, consist of dense concrete. The parking stalls lie on bands of pervious concrete, each 36 ft (11.0 m) wide.

The pervious-concrete slabs are 6 in. (150 mm) thick. A substantial reservoir underlies the pervious slabs, consisting of a 15 in. (380 mm) layer of coarse stone and recycled concrete, topped with recycled concrete meeting a #57 gradation. Perforated pipe drains are spaced 40 ft (12.2 m) apart.

The contractor used a telescoping belt conveyor to transport the pervious concrete from the ready-mix trucks to its final location. A laser screed with roller head leveled and compacted the fresh concrete. A four-person crew placed, on average, about 6000 sq ft (590 sq m) a day.

The pervious slabs do not contain crack-control joints. A few cracks have appeared, but they are far apart.

Cincinnati has a wet-freeze climate. But when I photographed the parking lot it was just a few months old and had yet to experience its first winter.

This parking lot at the Cincinnati Zoo contains alternating bands of dense and pervious concrete.

Joint between pervious and dense concrete at the Cincinnati Zoo.

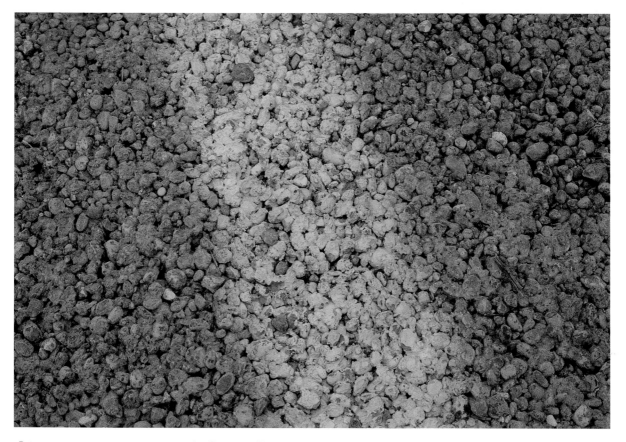

Paint stripe on pervious concrete at the Cincinnati Zoo.

An all-pervious parking lot

The designers of this parking lot, at the Oregon Trail Park in Olathe, Kansas, picked pervious concrete for the whole surface, not just the parking stalls.

Soil infiltration rates are low on this site, so stormwater is filtered through a wetland after passing through the pavement.

Joints were sawn on a close grid, but they did not prevent all cracks. The cracks are narrow and not easy to find. The concrete contains cellulose fibers.

Like the Cincinnati Zoo lot, this one was just a few months old when I photographed it in 2009, so its durability remains unknown. The climate falls in the hard-wet-freeze category.

The parking lot at the Oregon Trail Park in Olathe, Kansas, is all-pervious.

The Olathe pavement has cracked, but the cracks are not very obvious.

Joints in the Olathe parking lot look neat, but did not wholly succeed in preventing cracks.

Regular sweeping goes a long way toward preventing clogs. Look at how debris has collected in the corner the sweeper missed.

Glossary

Admixture — material added to a concrete mix, but not including cement, cement-replacement materials, aggregates, water, and fibers

Aggregate — rock particles

Aggregate interlock — process by which load is transferred across a joint or crack through direct contact between the aggregate particles on each side

Air entrainer — admixture used to make microscopic bubbles in cement paste, usually for the purpose of improving concrete's frost resistance

Base — pavement layer that supports asphalt, similar to the sub-base under a concrete slab

Block paver — masonry unit, pervious or impervious, used for paving

Cement — glue that binds the aggregates to form concrete

Cement-replacement material — pozzolan; powder that has some cementitious properties when blended with Portland cement

Clogging — filling of voids in pervious concrete with material such as leaf litter or silt

Coarse aggregate — rock particles at least 3/16 in. (5 mm) across

Cold joint — discontinuity in concrete caused by a delay in the pour or a change in the mix

Compaction — reduction of air spaces in soil, aggregate, or fresh concrete

Compressive strength — ability of a material to resist crushing

Concrete — construction material made of rock particles bound with cement; when used alone, the term usually refers to concrete made with Portland cement

Consolidation — compaction

Construction joint — seam between two concrete slabs cast at separate times

Contraction joint — break within a concrete slab intended to allow the concrete to contract or shrink without cracking

Crack — unplanned break in a concrete slab

Cross roller — long-handled roller used to compact pervious concrete at right angles to the main strike-off

Crushed rock — aggregate formed by artificially breaking rock

Curing — process of keeping fresh concrete moist so hydration can continue

Dense concrete — everyday concrete that includes fine aggregate; the term is normally used only when needed to distinguish this material from pervious concrete

Design rain event — the amount of water a pavement is designed to handle without overflowing

Detention pond — artificial depression in the landscape meant to store runoff for gradual release downstream or into the earth, but drying out between storms

Draindown — process in which cement paste or asphalt drips off the aggregate

Drawdown time — length of time needed for a reservoir to drain from full to empty

Drying shrinkage — concrete's reduction in volume as it dries out

Entrained air — small air bubbles intentionally introduced into concrete, usually to help resist frost damage

Expansion joint — break within a concrete slab, or between a slab and another structure, intended to allow the concrete to expand as temperature rises

Expansive clay — soil that swells greatly when wet

Fibers — short, flexible filaments added to the concrete mix, often made of polypropylene or cellulose

Filter fabric — sheet material with very small holes, meant to allow water through while blocking sand and silt; also called geotextile

Filtration — process by which pervious concrete separates solids from liquids

Fine aggregate — rock particles less than 3/16 in. (5 mm) across

Flexible pavement — pavement (usually asphalt) that transfers loads by compression to underlying layers that spread the stress

Flexural strength — ability of a material to resist bending

Fly ash — by-product of coal burning used as a cement-replacement material

Forms or formwork — mold into which fresh concrete is placed

Freeze-thaw cycle — temperature change that includes one fall below the freezing point and one rise back above it

Geomembrane — liner

Geotextile — filter fabric

Grading — process of bringing a surface (soil, sub-base, or concrete) to the desired elevation and slope

Gravel — coarse aggregate, especially that formed by natural processes and usually more rounded than crushed rock

Heat island — artificially warm area in the landscape, usually associated with cities

Hydration — chemical reactions involving cement and water that make concrete hard and strong

Hydration stabilizer — set stabilizer; admixture that markedly delays the setting of concrete

Hydrology — science of water, especially as it relates to rainfall

Infiltration — passing of water into a surface or into a distinct layer beneath the surface

Infiltration rate — speed with which water passes into a surface, usually expressed in inches or millimeters per hour

Isolation joint — separation between a concrete slab and another structure

Joint — planned break in a concrete slab or between a concrete slab and another structure

Joint filler — compressible board used to make expansion joints and isolation joints

Joint roller — long-handled roller with a fin that presses a groove into concrete, used for making joints

Laser Screed (trade name) — mechanized tool for striking-off, combined with a laser to establish grade

LEED — short for Leadership in Energy and Environmental Design, a program that awards points to construction projects for their contribution to sustainability and environmental protection

Liner — impervious sheet material used under some pavements; also called geomembrane

Load transfer — shifting of stress from the loaded side of a joint or crack to the unloaded side

No-fines concrete — concrete made without fine aggregate, nearly synonymous with pervious concrete and porous concrete

Pea gravel — coarse aggregate with particles about 3/8 in. (10 mm) across

Pervious — open to the transmission of water

Pervious asphalt — asphalt concrete made with little or no fine aggregate and containing connected voids that let water pass through

Pervious concrete — concrete made with little or no fine aggregate and containing connected voids that let water pass through, also called porous concrete

Pervious pavement — hard surface (not necessarily concrete) that is open to the transmission of water

Pizza cutter — joint roller; long-handled roller with a fin that presses a groove into concrete, used for making joints

Plasticizer — admixture that allows concrete to be made with less water while retaining workability; also called water reducer

Portland cement — cement made of clay and limestone, heated almost to melting and ground to a powder

Porous concrete — concrete made with little or no fine aggregate and containing connected voids that let water pass through; also called pervious concrete

Pozzolan — cement-replacement material such as fly ash or slag

Raveling — degradation of a pervious concrete surface in which aggregate particles break loose

Ready-mixed concrete — concrete made off site and delivered by truck

Reservoir — the part of a pervious pavement that stores water for gradual release into drains or subgrade

Recycled concrete — aggregate made by running old concrete through a rock crusher

Retarder — admixture that slows the setting of concrete

Retention pond — artificial body of water meant to store runoff and release it slowly downstream or into the ground

Rigid pavement — pavement (usually concrete) that transmits loads to the ground by its resistance to bending

Roller — heavy steel tube used to compact pervious concrete

Roller screed — motorized, spinning steel tube used for striking-off

Runoff — passing of water over a surface; the amount of water passed downhill

Screed — tool for striking-off

Sealing — closing of voids in pervious concrete, usually with cement paste

Set stabilizer — admixture that markedly delays the setting of concrete; also called hydration stabilizer

Shared-use path — way used by walkers and cyclists, and sometimes also by skaters and equestrians

Slab — the part of the pavement made of concrete

Slag — by-product of the steelmaking industry used as a cement-replacement material

Slope — deviation from a horizontal plane, usually expressed as the rise (vertical component) divided by the run (horizontal component)

Soakaway — hole in the ground, usually filled with unbound aggregate, from which stormwater can slowly drain

Solar reflectance index — a measure of how hot a material gets in sunshine

SRI — solar reflectance index, a measure of how hot a material gets in sunshine

Stormwater — water that makes its way through the landscape after originating as rainfall or snowmelt

Striking off — grading of fresh concrete, normally done by sliding a straight beam along the top of the forms; also called screeding

Subgrade — natural ground that supports a pavement

Sub-base — pavement layer between subgrade and slab

Swelling soil — expansive clay

Tamper — hand tool for compacting concrete, sub-base, or subgrade

Telebelt (trade name) — telescoping belt conveyor, used to place pervious concrete

Unbound aggregate — rock particles left loose, without cement, used as a sub-base or as an alternative to concrete or asphalt paving

Unit weight — density, expressed as pounds per cubic foot or kilogrammes per cubic meter

Vibrating screed — tool for striking-off that includes a vibrator to compact the concrete

Viscosity modifier — admixture that thickens the cement paste, reducing draindown

Void content — percentage of a concrete's volume not taken up by aggregate and cement

Water reducer — admixture that allows concrete to be made with less water while retaining workability; also called plasticizer

Wheelstop — raised strip used on parking lots to keep cars in position

White Portland cement — cement with a bright white color, otherwise similar to ordinary Portland cement

References

AASHTO, Guide for the Development of Bicycle Facilities, Washington, American Association of State Highway and Transportations Officials, 1999.

ACI 330R, Guide for the Design and Construction of Concrete Parking Lots, Farmington, Hills, Michigan, American Concrete Institute, 2003.

ACI 522R, Pervious Concrete, Farmington Hills, Michigan, American Concrete Institute, 2006.

Ashley, Erin, "Using Pervious Concrete to Earn LEED Points", *Concrete InFocus*, Winter 2008, 81-84.

ASTM C 33, Standard Specification for Concrete Aggregates, West Conshohocken, ASTM International, 2008.

ASTM C 1688, Standard Test Method for Density and Void Content of Freshly Mixed Pervious Concrete, West Conshohocken, ASTM International, 2008.

ASTM E 1980, Standard Practice for Calculating Solar Reflectance Index of Horizontal and Low-Sloped Opaque Surfaces, West Conshohocken, ASTM International, 2001.

Bradshaw, Anthony, Ben Hunt, and Tim Walmsley, *Trees in the Urban Landscape*, Cambridge, E and FN Spon, 1995.

Cottrell, Wayne D., "Development of Motorcycle Parking Design Guidelines", Proceedings of the 87th Annual Meeting of the Transportation Research Board, Jan. 2008, 3-4.

Delatte, Norbert, Dan Miller, and Aleksandar Mrkajic, Portland Cement Pervious Concrete Pavement: Field Performance Investigation on Parking Lot and Roadway Pavements, Report to the RMC Research and Education Foundation, 2007.

Enoch, M. D., *Concrete for Sports and Play Areas*, Wexham Springs, Cement and Concrete Association, 1976.

Enoch, M. D., *Concrete Bases for Non-Turf Cricket Pitches*, Wexham Springs, Cement and Concrete Association, 1980.

Ferguson, Bruce K., *Porous Pavements*, Boca Raton, Taylor & Francis, 2005

Freeze Thaw Resistance of Pervious Concrete, Silver Spring, Maryland, National Ready Mixed Concrete Association, 2004.

Higgins, Steve, Steve Workman, and Robert J. Coleman, *Pervious Concrete as a Flooring Material for Horse Handling Areas*, Lexington, University of Kentucky, 2007.

Lichter, John M., and Patricia A. Lindsey, "Soil Compaction and Site Construction", *The Landscape Below Ground*, Savoy, Illinois, International Society of Arboriculture, 1994, 126-130.

Luck, Joe David, Effect of Pervious Concrete on Potential Environmental Impacts from Animal Production Facilities, Thesis, University of Kentucky, 2007.

Maynard, D. P., "A Fine No-Fines Road", *Concrete Construction*, April 1970, 116-117.

"McD Concrete Enterprises Places Large Pervious Job", *Voice of the Concrete Contractor*, May 2009, 1.

Murdock, L. J., K. M. Brook, and J. D. Dewar, *Concrete Materials and Practice*, Sixth Edition, London, Edward Arnold, 1991.

Roadway Lighting, New York, Illuminating Engineering Society of North America, 1983.

Rolf, Kaj, "Soil Compaction and Loosening Effects on Soil Physics and Tree Growth", *The Landscape Below Ground*, Savoy, Illinois, International Society of Arboriculture, 1994, 131-148.

Stark, Richard E., "Road Surface's Reflectance Influences Lighting Design", *Lighting Design + Application*, April 1986, 42-26.

Schaefer, Vernon, Keijin Wang, Muhannad T. Suleiman, and John T. Kevern, *Mix Design Development for Pervious Concrete in Cold Weather Climates*, Ames, Iowa, Iowa State University, 2006.

Sparkman, Alan, Tennessee Concrete Association, interview on 7 October 2009.

Tennis, Paul D., Michael L. Leming, and David J. Akers, *Pervious Concrete Pavements*, Skokie, Portland Cement Association, 2004.

Valore, Rudolph C., Jr., and William C. Green, "Air Replaces Sand in 'No-Fines' Concrete", Proceeding of the American Concrete Institute, Detroit, American Concrete Institute, 1951.

Index